Also available:

But I'm a Gilmore!

STORIES AND EXPERIENCES OF CAST, CREW, AND FANS

TARYN DRYFHOUT

You've Been Gilmored!

A CULTURAL REFERENCE GUIDE

TARYN DRYFHOUT

THE UNOFFICIAL ENCYCLOPEDIA OF
DESPERATE HOUSEWIVES

THE UNOFFICIAL ENCYCLOPEDIA OF
DESPERATE HOUSEWIVES

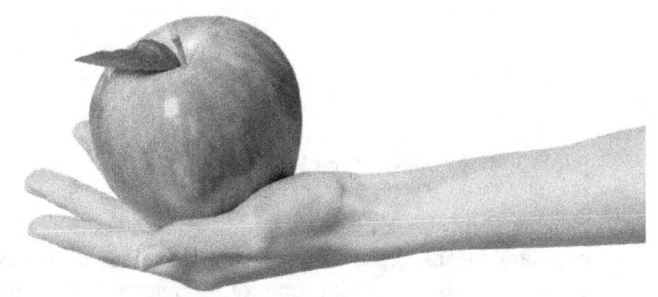

The Comprehensive Cultural Reference Guide

by Taryn Dryfhout

Although the author has made every effort to ensure that the information in this book was correct at the time of print, the author does not assume and hereby disclaim any liability to any party for any loss, damage, or disruption caused by errors or omissions, whether such errors or omissions result from neglig

Published by Bluestocking Books NZ.

No part of this book may be reproduced or transmitted in any form or by any means, electronic or mechanical, including photocopying or recording, or by any information storage and retrieval system, without permission in writing from the publisher.

All photos and/or copyrighted material appearing in this book remains the work of its owners. Every effort has been made to give credit. No infringement is intended in this work. The title of this work, "Desperate for Housewives", as well as most of the chapter titles are phrases from *Desperate Housewives* and are not owned by the author. This book is not official, authorised by, or affiliated with ABC Studios, Cherry Productions, or their representatives.

ISBN 978 0 473 63970 9

First Published 2022. © All Rights Reserved.

Second Edition.

For all those who live lives of quiet desperation

Contents

Introduction..11

Quiet Desperation: About the Show..............................15

- Opening Credit Sequence...16
- Episode List..24
- Character List...32
- *Desperate Housewives* Referenced In....................44
- Themed Episode Lists...54
- Awards and Nominations..59
- Desperate Housewives by the Numbers..................67

Noisy Fulfillment: A Reference Guide.........................68

- Love and Relationships...69
- List of Secrets on the Show...................................116
- Documents..140
- Movies 159
- Musicals and Theatre..166
- Television...168
- Music...171
- Literature..177
- Illnesses..194
- Sports and Games...198
- Animals and Pets..202
- Oakridge animal groups..203
- Charade groups..204
- Bree and Rex Control word ideas (1.14) 204

Suburbia is a battleground: Eagle State, Fairview, and Wisteria Lane..205

- Fairview, Eagle State..206
- Wisteria Lane...209
- Mapping Wisteria Lane..232
- Business Directory...234
- Events..249
- Places..255

**"How much do we really want to know about our neighbors?":
Trivia**...269

References and Credits..287

Introduction

A Desperate Housewife

When people ask me why *Desperate Housewives* holds such an important place in my heart, I tell them it is because of how formative this show was for me. When it first aired in October of 2004, I had been married for only six months. I was still working out the kinks, and the rhythm of married life, and trying to establish what kind of housewife I wanted to be. Like housewives everywhere, I suddenly found the experiences and concerns of my own life and marriage reflected back, in the lives of these 'desperate' women that we watched navigate love, loss, and everything in-between. I am a fan of several different television shows, but *Desperate Housewives* hit me differently. I resonated with qualities and storylines from multiple characters, and allowed this show to embed itself in my identity. I became a desperate housewife in 2004, and I have never looked back.

The Cultural Impact of Desperate Housewives

The popularity of the show while it was on air, cannot be overstated. The pilot clocked up an audience of 22 million when it aired in 2004, and went on to average 21 million viewers per episode. The actors on the show graced the cover of every major magazine, every red carpet, and billboards all over the world. Even my town in New Zealand had billboards on skyscrapers, with the women of Wisteria Lane. First Lady Laura Bush confessed to being a huge fan of the show, and Oprah ran a special called "Wisteria Hysteria". The show was sold to most major television markets around the world, and made instant stars out of the main cast. Books were even written about the show "to understand why a seemingly harmless, darkly comedic soap opera should prove an instant ratings winner – and immediately stir up controversy. Only on air for a few weeks and it was already a pop culture phenomenon".

This impact extended to the television industry in a wider sense than just ratings. *Desperate Housewives* put mystery shows on the map. The hybridity of its construction made the show the first of its kind, and blazed the trailer for so many other shows to follow such as *Pretty Little Liars*, *Big Little Lies, and Little Fires Everywhere*. *Desperate Housewives* showed a blackly comic vision of suburban life that other shows had not dared to enter. Rosalind Coward writes that,

> "Behind the perfect façade, with immaculate houses, clean streets, perfectly tended lawns and apparently perfect families, there is obsession, malevolence, frustration and above all secrets – people hiding things from each other and themselves." (2)

There is an uncanniness about the show that was not preceded on television. The housewives on the show are real - they laugh, they cry, they hide bodies in the freezer, and bury them in the woods. The show opens with a deceased narrator, but then quickly shows Martha Huber seeing the silver lining of this senseless tragedy. The tradition of shows that followed, which juggled these light and dark elements, owe a substantial debt to *Desperate Housewives*.

What This Book Is

While there have been books written about *Desperate Housewives*, to date there has not been an encyclopedia that catalogs the show. This book is not intended to help you get to know the actors behind the series or how the set operates. This book is intended to be a comprehensive compendium of everything that is referenced, and takes place within the world of the show - including every secret and lie ever told on the show, every affair, every death. You will also find out everything you have ever wanted to know about the world of

Fairview and Wisteria Lane and the colorful characters and events that inhabit it.

The bulk of the book takes the form of 'lists'. These lists document all of the movies, television shows, music, food, and books that were referenced throughout *Desperate Housewives*. This book also contains lists of all of the pets that featured in the series, the businesses and events that made up the unique town of Fairview and Wisteria Lane, as well as every illness, geographical place ever mentioned on the show, and so much more.

The book opens with a comprehensive episode list—detailing the season, episode number, and title. After the episode list, each episode mentioned throughout the book will be marked by its season, and episode in numeral form. For example, a reference to episode five of season six, will simply be marked as (6.5).

The Trivia section, as well as many of the lists, are designed to accompany a re-watch of the show. Each episode is numbered with interesting information about each episode. Lists such as the Relationship Guide, or the Fairview Town Guide are designed for reference, and of course, interest.

It probably goes without saying, but this book is loaded with spoilers, and is intended for reading only after an initial watch of the show. Even reading along with the trivia section at the same time as watching, will likely reveal spoilers, as I provide connections to characters and story arcs which appear later in the show.

It is also necessary at this point to draw attention to the fact that this book has no official, or authorized connection to the show, or ABC. This work was fan-produced, from multiple re-watches of the show and from critical research of the show. References to the show are explicit throughout, usually by the accompaniment of an episode reference (e.g. 7.2). All chapter titles are references to quotes used throughout the show, and remain the work of the copyright owner.

It is my sincere hope that reading this book, and in using it as a companion to the show that you will find this encyclopedia helpful, and that it will enrich, and enhance your enjoyment of the show. While every care has been taken to ensure that this guide is as accurate, and comprehensive as possible, I would love to hear if you think I have missed anything that could be included in any subsequent reprints of this book. (anotherdesperatehousewife@gmail.com).

It is impossible to articulate how much a part of my life *Desperate Housewives* has become, and I know that fans all over the world have felt the same since the show first aired in 2004. Theodore Roosevelt once said "I am a part of everything that I have ever read". I believe this is true, but I want to extend this to include films and television shows, because I know that I am a part of *Desperate Housewives*, as much as it has become a part of who I am.

Taryn

QUIET DESPERATION
ABOUT THE SHOW

Opening Credit Sequence

The quirky opening credits for *Desperate Housewives* are made up of a sequence of images derived from famous artworks which all speak to the role of women in society, and in marriage. It is clear from this opening sequence, which references relationships throughout history, that this is a show like no other. Each of the artworks demonstrate a woman who is desperate in her own way, but collectively points to the female-oriented narrative that we are about to watch.

The following artworks are included in the title sequence:

- "Adam and Eve"
- The Tomb Paintings of Queen Nefertari
- "The Arnolfini Portrait"
- "American Gothic"
- "Pin Up Girl"
- "Am I Proud!"
- "Campbell's Soup Cans"
- "Romantic Couple"
- "Couple Arguing"

Adam and Eve - Lucas Cranach the Elder

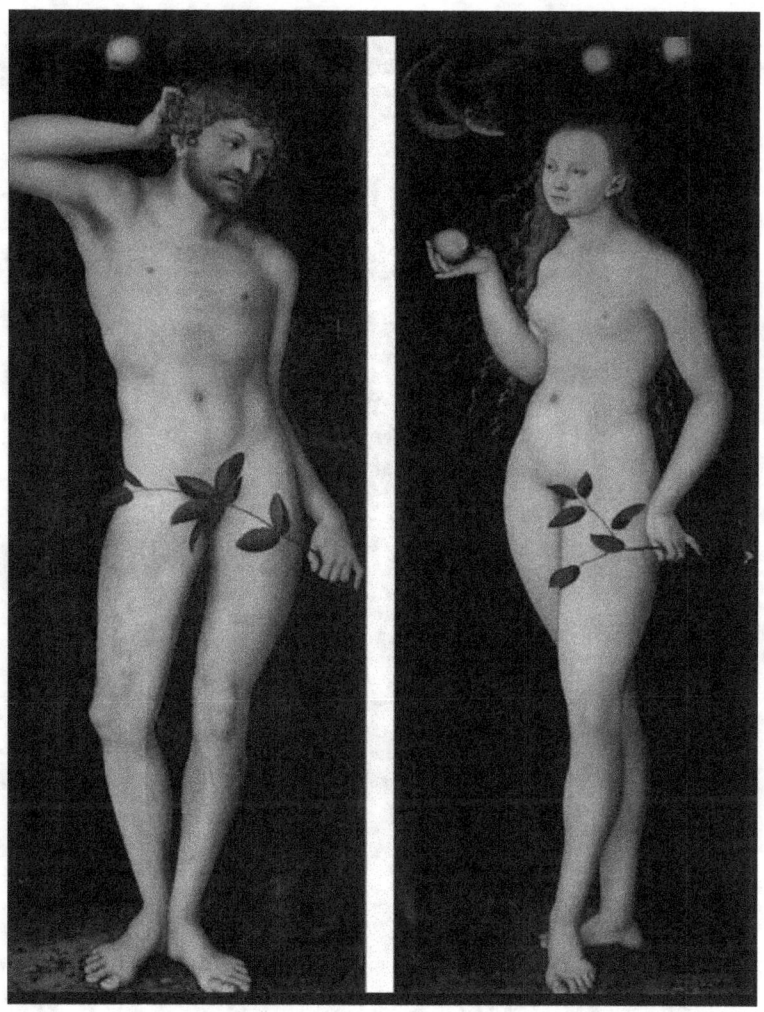

The Tomb Paintings of Queen Nefertari

The Arnolfini Portrait - Jan Van Eyck

American Gothic - Grant Wood

Pin Up Girl - Gil Elvgren

Am I Proud - Dick Williams

Campbell's Soup Cans - Andy Warhol

Romantic Couple - Robert Dale

Couple Arguing - Robert Dale

Episodes

Season One

1. Pilot
2. Ah, But Underneath
3. Pretty Little Picture
4. Who's That Woman?
5. Come In, Stranager
6. Running to Stand Still
7. Anything You Can Do
8. Guilty
9. Suspicious Minds
10. Come Back to Me
11. Move On
12. Every Day a Little Death
13. Your Fault
14. Love Is in the Air
15. Impossible
16. The Ladies Who Lunch
17. There Won't Be Trumpers
18. Children Will Listen
19. Live Alone and Like It
20. Fear No More
21. Sunday in the Park with George
22. Goodbye for Now
23. One Wonderful Day

Season Two

1. Next
2. You Could Drive a Person Crazy
3. You'll Never Get Away from Me
4. My Heart Belongs to Daddy
5. They Asked Me Why I Believe in You
6. I Wish I Could Forget You
7. Color and Light
8. The Sun Won't Set
9. That's Good, That's Bad
10. Coming Home
11. One More Kiss
12. We're Gonna Be All Right
13. There's Something About a War
14. Silly People
15. Thank You So Much
16. There is No Other Way
17. Could I Leave You?
18. Everybody Says Don't
19. Don't Look at Me
20. It Wasn't Meant to Happen
21. I Know Things Now
22. No One is Alone
23. Remember

Season Three

1. Listen to the Rain on the Roof
2. It Takes Two
3. A Weekend in the Country
4. Like It Was
5. Nice She Ain't
6. Sweetheart, I Have to Confess
7. Bang
8. Children and Art
9. Beautiful Girls
10. The Miracle Song
11. No Fits, No Fights, No Feuds
12. Not While I'm Around
13. Come Play Wiz Me
14. I Remember That
15. The Little Things You Do Together
16. My Husband, the Pig
17. Dress Big
18. Liaisons
19. God, That's Good
20. Gossip
21. Into the Woods
22. What Would We Do Without You?
23. Getting Married Today

Season Four

1. Now You Know
2. Smiles of a Summer Night
3. The Game
4. If There's Anything I Can't Stand
5. Art Isn't Easy
6. Now I Know, Don't Be Scared
7. You Can't Judge a Book By Its Cover
8. A Distant Past
9. Something's Coming
10. Welcome to Kanagawa
11. Sunday
12. In Buddy's Eyes
13. Hello, Little Girl
14. Opening Doors
15. Mother Said
16. The Gun Song
17. Free

Season Five

1. You're Gonna Love Tomorrow
2. We're So Happy You're So Happy
3. Kids Ain't Like Everybody Else
4. Back in Business
5. Mirror, Mirror
6. There's Always a Woman
7. What More Do I Need?
8. City on Fire
9. Me and My Town
10. A Vision's Just a Vision
11. Home Is the Place
12. Connect! Connect!
13. The Best Thing That Ever Could Have Happened
14. Mama Spent Money When She Had None
15. In a World Where the Kings Are Employers
16. Crime Doesn't Pay
17. The Story of Lucy and Jessie
18. A Spark. To Pierce the Dark.
19. Look Into THeir Eyes and You See What They Know
20. Rose's Turn
21. Bargaining
22. Marry Me a Little
23. Everybody Says Don't
24. If It's Only In Your Head

Season Six

1. Nice Is Different Than Good
2. Being Alive
3. Never Judge a Lady By Her Lover
4. The God-Why-Don't-You-Love-Me Blues
5. Everybody Ought to Have a Maid
6. Don't Walk on the Grass
7. Careful the Things You Say
8. The Coffee Cup
9. Would I Think of Suicide?
10. Boom Crunch
11. If…
12. You Gotta Get a Gimmick
13. How About a Friendly Shrink?
14. The Glamorous Life
15. Lovely
16. The Chase
17. Chromolume No. 7
18. My Two Young Men
19. We All Deserve to Die
20. Epiphany
21. A Little Night Music
22. The Ballad of Booth
23. I Guess This Is Goodbye

Season Seven

1. Remember Paul?
2. You Must Meet My Wife
3. Truly Content
4. The Thing That Counts Is What's Inside
5. Let Me Entertain You
6. Excited and Scared
7. A Humiliating Business
8. Sorry Grateful
9. Pleasant Little Kingdom
10. Down the Block There's a Riot
11. Assassins
12. Where Do I Belong
13. I'm Still Here
14. Flashback
15. Farewell Letter
16. Searching
17. Everything's Different, Nothing's Changed
18. Moments in the Woods
19. The Lies Ill-Concealed
20. I'll Swallow Poison on Sunday
21. Then I really Got Scared
22. And Lots of Security…
23. Come on Over for Dinner

Season Eight

1. Secrets That I Never Want to Know
2. Making the Connection
3. Watch While I Revise the World
4. School of Hard Knocks
5. The Art of Making Art
6. Witch's Lament
7. Always in Control
8. Suspicion Song
9. Putting It Together
10. What's to Discuss, Old Friend
11. Who Can Say What's True?
12. What's the Good of Being Good
13. Is This What You Call Love?
14. Get Out of My Life
15. She Needs Me
16. You Take for Granted
17. Women and Death
18. Any Moment
19. With So Little to Be Sure Of
20. Lost My Power
21. The People Will Hear
22. Give Me the Blame
23. Finishing the Hat

Character List

8-Year-Old Boy
Mary Ann
AA Member
Accountant
Addison Prudy
Adele Delfino
Administrator
Agency Model
Agent Aronson
Agent Jackson
Agent Pedilla
Airline Passenger
Al Kaminsky
Alan
Alan - Paramedic
Alan Marcus
Alberta Fromme
Alberta Holstein
Alcoholic Neighbor
Alejandro
Alexandra
Alfred the Orderly
Alisa Stevens
Allen
Allison Scavo
Ally
Alma Hodge
Altar Boy
Alvin Portsmouth, Mediator
Amanda
Amber James

Amy Pearce
Amy Yamada
Ana Solis
Andre Zeller
Andrew Buddy
Andrew Buddy #2
Andrew Van De Kamp
Andrew's Dancer
Angel
Angie Bolen
Animal handler trainer
Annabel Foster
Anne Peterson
Anne Schilling
Annie Marie
Antony
Arnold
Arresting Police Officer
Art Shepherd
Ashley Bukowski
Asian Woman
Attendant
Attorney
Audrey
Aunt Fern
Austin McCann
Baby Lilly
Baby Mayer
Babysitter
Background
Bar Patron

Barbara Fine
Barbara Orlofsky
Barista
Barrett
Barry
Bart
Bartender
Bartender in Biker Bar
Bartender in Dance Club
Beefy Middle-Aged Woman
Bellman
Ben Faulkner
Benjamin Katz
Bermuda Tourist
Bernice
Bertollini Brother #1
Bess
Best man
Beth Young
Bethany
Betty
Betty Applewhite
Betty's Conductor
Betty's Piano Teacher
Biker Babe
Bartender
Bikini Girl
Bill

Bill Brown
Bill Cunningham
Bill Pearce
Blood Drive Nurse
Board Chairman
Board Leader
Bob
Bob Fisk
Bob Hunter
Bob Rowland
Booking Sergeant
Boomer
Boot Camp Trainee
Bouncer
Box Boy
Boy #1
Boy #2
Boy #3
Boy (Face Paint)
Boy Getting Candy to Sell
Boy on Bike
Boy with Flowers
Boy with Santa Claus
Bradley
Bradley Scott
Brandi
Brandon
Bree Hodge
Bree Van De Kamp
Bree's Friend
Bree's Laughing Dinner Guest

Bree's Lawyer
Bree's Mother
Bree's Neighbor
Bree's Nurse
Brent Ferguson
Brett
Brian
Brian Linder
Bride
Brittney
Bruce
Bryan
Bud Penrod
Bum
Burton
Bus Driver
Busboy
Businessman
Bystander
Cab Driver
Cabaret Show Patron
Cabbie
Cable Guy
Caleb Applewhite
Callie
Camp Hennessey Kid
Campaign Rally Introducer
Candace
Car Salesman
Carjacker
Carl
Carlos Solis
Carmen
Carmen Luna
Carmen Sanchez

Carol Prudy
Carolyn Bigsby
Carter
Cashier
Casting Director
Caterer
Ceal
Cecile the Stripper
Celia Solis
Chad
Charlene
Charles Babcock
Charles McLain
Charles Skouras
Charlie
Charlie James
Charlotte Fletcher
Cheerleader
Cheerleader
Child
Child Pilgrim
Chinese Girl
Chloe
Christina
Christmas Choir Member
Chuck
Chuck Vance
Cindy
City Councilwoman
Civil War Major
Claire
Claire Bremmer
Claire Cormier
Claude
Claudia Sanchez

Clay
Clerk
Clinic Doctor
Clown
Club Member
Clubber
Clyde
Coach
Coach Wilkins
Cocktail Waiter
Coco the Clown
Coffee Shop Patron
Colleen Henderson
College Professor
College Student
Conference Executive
Connie Solis
Connie Thomas
Construction Driver
Construction Guy
Cop
Cop #1
Coroner
Cosmetic Store Customer
Costumer
Country Club Maitre D'
Court Room Lawyer
Courtroom Reporter
Cowboy
Cowgirl Waitress
Craig Lynwood

Crime Scene Policeman
Crossing Guard
Crystal
Cub Scout
Curtis Monroe
Customer
Cute New Yorker
Cyrus
D.A. Stone
Dahlia Hainsworth
Dakota
Dale Helm
Damon
Dan
Dana
Dancer
Danielle Van De Kamp
Danny Bolen
Danny Farrel
Daphne Bicks
Darcy
Daughter-in-Law
Dave Koz
Dave Williams
David Bradley
Dealer
Deanna
Debbie
Debby
Debi Brown
Deborah Gotlieb
Deirdre
Deirdre Taylor
Delivery Guy
Delivery Man
Delores Mason

Denise
Dennis Stevens
Derek
Derek Yeager
Detective
Detective #2
Detective Aguilar
Detective Anson
Detective Barton
Detective Beckerman
Detective Berry
Detective Bryant
Detective Burnett
Detective Collins
Detective Copeland
Detective Denise Lapera
Detective Fallon
Detective Foster
Detective Furst
Detective Gillette
Detective Hank Powell
Detective Harrison
Detective Heredia
Detective Hewitt
Detective John Booth
Detective Lyons
Detective Murphy
Detective Paul Bullock
Detective Ridley

Detective Romslow	Dr. Baker	Dr. Wagner
Detective Schroeder	Dr. Baron	Dr. Wheeler
Detective Shrank	Dr. Barr	Dr. Wyner
Detective Sloan	Dr. Berman	Driver
Detective Sullivan	Dr. Bernstein	Durki
Detective Turner	Dr. Brody	Dylan
Detective in Hallway	Dr. Chang	Dylan Mayfair
Diane	Dr. Claude Kyl	EMT
Dick Barrows	Dr. Craig	EMT #1
Dick Jackson	Dr. Crane2 epis	EMT Gurneyman for Lillian Sims
Doctor	Dr. Cunningham	ER Doctor
Doctor L. Sage	Dr. David Griffith	Ed Ferrara
Doctor Shiller	Dr. Delson	Eddie
Dominick	Dr. Fitzgerald	Eddie Orlofsky
Don	Dr. Gainsburg	Edgar
Donald	Dr. Graham	Edie Britt
Donna	Dr. Hanson	Edna
Donnie	Dr. Henry Gable	Edwin Hodge
Donny	Dr. Hill	Eileen
Doreen Vance	Dr. Jenkins	Eileen Britt
Doris	Dr. Joshua Dolan	Elderly Lady
Doris Hammond	Dr. Kagan	Eleanor Garrett
Double D Club Patron	Dr. Lippman	Eleanor Mason
Doug	Dr. Lunt	Elegant Woman
Doug Perry	Dr. Manning	Eli Scruggs
Dowager	Dr. Martin	Elizabeth
Dr. Adam Mayfair	Dr. Mary Wagner	Ellie Leonard
Dr. Albert Goldfine	Dr. McCarthy	Emcee
Dr. Alex Cominis	Dr. McLean	Emily Portsmith
Dr. Avedon	Dr. Oakley	Emma Graham
Dr. Bach	Dr. Peters	Emma Graham's Daughter
Dr. Bailey	Dr. Ron McCready	Eric
	Dr. Rushton	Erica
	Dr. Samuel Heller	Erika Gold
	Dr. Sicher	Ethan
	Dr. Sugarman	Eugene Beale
		Evan Mayer

Evelyn	Frank Helm	Girl with Packages
Ex-Con	Frank Kaminsky	Glen Wingfield
Exterminator	Frank Sweeney	Glenn Morris
Extra	François	Gloria Hodge
FBI Agent	Fred Newman	Gold Digger
Father	Freddy	Gordie
Father Benson	Friedrich	Gossipy Woman
Father Crowley	Frustrated Customer	Gotlieb Friend
Father Drance	Funeral Attendee	Grace
Father Dugan	Funeral Attendee	Grace Sanchez
Featured	Funeral Director	Graham
Featured Waitress	Funeral Guest	Hainsworth
Felicia Tilman	Funny Trick-or-Treater	Grandmother Manzani
Felix Bergman	Gabrielle Solis	Greg
Female Guard	Gangbanger #1	Greg Limon
Female Jewelry Clerk	Garage Sale Shopper	Groom
Female Prison Guard	Garbage Man	Groomsman
Fern Parrish	Garbage Truck Driver	Guard
Field Reporter	Gardener	Gus
Figurine Collecting Plumbing Customer	Gary	Gus, the Janitor
	Gary Grantham	Guy
	Gay Bar Patron	Guy #1
	Gayle	Guy #2
Fire Investigator	Geoffrey Mathers	Gwen
Fireman	George Williams	Haggard Woman
Flight Attendant	Gil	Handsome Man
Football Coach	Gilbert McCluskey	Handsome Stranger
Football Man	Gillian	Hank
Football Player	Ginger	Hank Orlofsky
Founder's Day Guest	Girl	Harlan Copp
Fran Ferrara	Girl Scout	Harry Gaunt
Fran Schulman	Girl With Dog	Harvey Bigsby
Francine Williams	Girl in restroom	Head Volunteer
Frank		Headmaster
		Lentz
		Hector

Hector 'The Ice Cream Man'
Hector Ramos
Hector Sanchez
Heidi Klum
Helen
Helen Rowland
Helen Vale
Helena
Henry Mason
Herbert Brickmeyer
High School Student
Hillary
Hipster
Homeless
Homeless Man
Homeless Woman
Hospital Nurse
Hospital Patient
Hospital Visitor
Hostess
Hot Guy 2 in Dance Club
Hot Guy in Dance Club
Hot Male Club Goer
Housekeeper
Housewife #1
Housewife #2
Howard Keck
Husband
IRS Agent
Ian Hainsworth
Ice Cream Vendor

Ida Greenberg
Ida's Neighbor
Immigration Agent
Immigration Agent #2
Inmate #1
Inmate #2
Inmate #3
Instructor
Investigator
Irene Semanis
Irina Kosokov
Iris Beckley
Isabel
Italian Secretary
Ivana
Jack
Jack Pinkham
Jackson Braddock
Jail Cell Officer
Jake Walker
Jane Carlson
Jane Hainsworth
Janie Peterson
Jason
Jasper Zeller
Jean
Jeff
Jeff Bicks
Jeffrey
Jeffrey Scott
Jennie Hernandez
Jennifer
Jennifer Morelli
Jenny

Jenny Hunter-McDermott
Jerome
Jerry
Jerry the Coroner
Jessie
Jewelry Clerk
Jill
Jill Newman
Jim Halverson
Jim Peterson
Jimbo Rooney
Jimmy
Jimmy Harper
Jodi
Jody
Joey Murphy
Jogger
John
John Rowland
Jonathan Lithgow
Jordana Geist
Jorge
Joyce
Joyce O'Hare
Juanita 'Mama' Solis
Juanita Solis
Judge
Judge Conti
Judge Mary Gallagher
Judge Sullivan
Judge Sullivan
Judy
Julie Mayer
Julie's Friend #1

Julie's Friend #2
Juror #1
Justice of the Peace
Justin
Karen
Karen McCluskey
Karl Mayer
Karl's Break-Up Girlfriend
Karl's Ex-Girlfriend #2
Karl's Ex-Girlfriend #3
Katherine Mayfair
Kayla Huntington
Keith Kavendish
Keith Watson
Kelli
Kelly
Ken
Kendra Taylor
Kent
Keri
Kevin
Kid
Kid Sister
Killer
Kim
Kimberly
Kirby Schilling
Kirstin
Kyle
Lab Technician
Lady
Lamar Benjamin

Lamar the Limo Driver
Lamont
Lance
Larry
Laura Delfino
Laura Miller
Lauren
Lauren Baxter
Lawyer
Lazaro
Lea Rappaport
Lee McDermott
Leila Mitzman
Leo Katz
Leonard Harper
Li Wang
Libby Collins
Lila Dash
Lillian Allen
Lillian Sims
Lily Stevens
Linda Flanagan
Lindsay
Lisa
Little Boy
Little Bully
Little Girl
Little Robin Hood
Lloyd
Local Pub Waiter
Lois McDaniel
Lonny Moon
Lori Jean
Lori Jean's Son
Louis
Lucia
Lucy

Lucy Blackburn
Luis
Luke Purdue
Luke Rayfield
Lupe
Lydia Lindquist
Lynette Scavo
Lynn Dean
M.J. Delfino
MJ's friend
MRI Technician
Madeline
Maggie Gilroy
Mahoney
Maid
Mailman
Maisy Gibbons
Makeup Artist
Malcolm
Male Model
Male News Anchor
Male Opera Singer
Male Stripper
Mall Security Guard
Man
Man at Mattress Store
Man in Church
Man in Pizzeria
Man in Truck
Man in Wheelchair #2
Manzani Sister
Marc
Marcella
Maria

Maria Scott
Mariana
Marilyn
Marisa Mayer
Marisa Sanchez
Market Customer
Martha Huber
Mary Alice Young
Mary Alice Young
Mary Beth
Maternity Nurse
Matt
Matthew Applewhite
Maureen
Maxine Bennett
Maxine Bennett's Friend
Maxine Rosen
Maya
Mayor Franklin
Mayor Johnson
Mayor's Lawyer
Medical Examiner
Meg Butler
Megan
Megan, Young woman
Melanie Foster
Melina Cominis
Melissa
Mia
Michelle
Michelle Downing
Mickey Gibb
Middle Aged Man
Middle-Aged Woman
Mike Delfino
Mike's Nurse
Millie
Milton Lang
Mimi
Minister
Miss Charlotte
Mitzi Kinsky
Moderator
Mohel
Molly
Mona Clark
Monique Polier
Monroe Carter
Morty Flickman
Mother
Mover
Moving Man
Mr. Bederman
Mr. Bowman
Mr. Chase
Mr. Dinsmore
Mr. Doyle
Mr. Falati
Mr. Fishman
Mr. Flannery
Mr. Franklin
Mr. Hartley
Mr. Jacobs
Mr. Jameson
Mr. Katzburg
Mr. Matthews
Mr. Pashmutt
Mr. Roarke
Mr. Scully
Mr. Shaw
Mr. Sim's Son
Mr. Steinberg
Mr. Stevens
Mr. Vivinetto
Mrs. Bukowski
Mrs. Epstein
Mrs. Horowitz
Mrs. Howe
Mrs. Kowalsky
Mrs. McKeever
Mrs. Novak
Mrs. Pate
Mrs. Templeton
Mrs. Tomlinson
Mrs. Truesdale
Ms. Elenora Butters
Ms. McCready
Muriel
Museum Visitor
Nabila
Nabila's Husband
Nanny
Natalie Klein
Neidermeyer
Neighbor
Neighbor with Dog
News Reporter
Newscaster
Nick
Nick Bolen
Nick Delfino
Nicy
Night Manager
Nikki
Nina Fletcher
Noah Taylor

Noah's Doctor
Nora Huntington
Norma Harper
Nun
Nurse
Nurse #2
Nurse Abagail
Nurse Kelly
Nurse Parker
Nurse Ruth Ann Heisel
Nurse Wilkins
Office Aide
Office Employee
Officer
Officer Brovka
Officer Daniels
Officer Ramsey
Officer Rick Thompson
Officer Ted Kreiger
Old Man
Older Gentleman
Older Man
Older Patrick
Older Woman
Oliver Weston
On Site TV Reporter
Online Customer
Opera Patron
Orderly
Orgasmic Feet
Orson Hodge
Owen Johnson
Padma
Pageant Emcee
Paige Dash

Paige Scavo
Pall-Bearer
Paramedic
Parent
Parishioner
Park Athlete
Park Bully
Park Ranger
Parker Scavo
Party Friend
Party Guest
Pat Ziegler
Patient
Patrick
Patrick Logan
Patti Jackson
Patty
Patty Rizzo
Paul Young
Paulina Porizkova
Pedestrian
Pedicurist #1
Pedicurist #2
Peggy
Penny Scavo
Perfect Swedish Man
Peter
Peter Hickey
Peter McMillan
Pharmacist
Phil
Phil Lopez
Phil the Tile Guy
Philo
Phong
Photographer

Phyllis Van De Kamp
Pianist
Pierced Juror
Pizza Ctomer
Pizza Parlor
Patron
Police Captain
Police Clerk
Police Officer
Police Officer #1
Policeman
Policewoman
Porter Scavo
Postman
Pregnant Woman #1
Pregnant Woman #2
Pregnant Woman #3
Prep School Mom
Preston Scavo
Principal Gomez
Principal Harris
Principal Hobson
Principal Stark
Prison Inmate
Prisoner
Property Manager
Prosecutor
Prostitute
Protester
Protestor #1
Psychiatric Patient
Rachel

Rachel - Crying Girl	Roberta Simmons	Secretary
Rachel Miller	Robin Gallagher	Security Guard
Ralph	Rodney Scavo	Self
Ramona	Roger	Self Defense Instructor
Ranger #2	Ron	Serena
Ranger Thompson	Rose	Sergeant Clemente
Raymond	Rose DeLuca	Sexy Jogger
Realtor	Rose Kemper	Sgt. Willems
Rebecca	Roy Bender	Shayla Grove
Rebecca Groves	Roy Harding	Sheila
Rebecca Shepard	Rupert	Sheriff
Receptionist	Russell	Sherri Maltby
Reggie	Russian Vodka Executive	Shirtless Man
Renee	Ryan Vayo	Shonda
Renee Perry	Sales Clerk	Shopper
Renee's Date	Saleslady	Shuttle Driver
Repo Man	Salesperson	Sid
Reporter	Saleswoman	Silvio Vitale
Reporter #2	Sally	Sister Marta
Reporter #3	Salon Customer	Sister Mary Bernard
Restaurant Patron	Salsa Dancer	Skanky Woman
Reverend	Sam	Skeevy Man
Reverend Green	Sam Allen	Sleazy Suit Patron
Reverend Lawson	Sam Killian	Sobbing Man
Reverend Sikes	Samantha Lang	Sobbing Woman
Rex Van De Kamp	Samuel Bormanis	Soccer Buddy
Rex's Lawyer	Sandra Birch	Socialite
Rhoda	Sarah	Solis Family Member
Richard	Scavo's Waiter	Son
Richard Watson	Scooter Girl	Son-in-Law
Rick Coletti	Scott	Sophie
Riot Protestor	Scott McKinney	Sophie Bremmer
Rita	Scott Tollman	Soprano Singer
Rita Patterson	Scout Leader	Stacy Strauss
Rita Rivara	Seamstress	
	Second Priest	
	Second Stripper	

Stagehand	Tennis Girl	Uniformed Cop
Stan	Teresa Pruitt	Unkempt Man
Stan	Terrence	Va Va Broom
Stan Grazi	Terrence	Ladies
Steel Worker	Henderson	Valet
Steel Worker	Texting Girl	Vanessa
Stella Wingfield	Texting Student	Vendor
Stephanie	The Adjustor	Vera Keck
Stephanie Lynne	The Counselor	Vern
Steve	Theresa Vitale	Veronica
Steven	Thief	Veterinarian
Stockboy	Thomas	Victor Lang
Street Kid	Thug #1	Victor Lang
Street Musician	Tiffany	Admirer
Strip Club Patron	Tim	Violet
Stripper	Tim Duggan	Virginia
Stripper Barbie	Tish Atherton	Hildebrand
Stu Durber	Toby	Visitor
Student	Tom Scavo	Waiter
Student	Tommy	Waitress
Supervisor	Toni	Wally
Susan Mayer	Tony	Walter
Swim Team Boy	Toph	Walter Bergen
Swimmer	Tracy Miller	Walter Bierlich
Sylvia Greene	Trainer	Warden
Tad	Transgender	Warren Schilling
Tad, Waiter	Translator	Water Glass
Tammy Brennan	Transsexual	Player
Tammy Rowland	Travers McLain	Wayne Davis
Tanaka Party	Trial Attendant	Wedding Guest
Waiter	Trip Weston	Wedding Party
Tanya	Trishelle	Guest
Teacher	Trumpet Player	Wendy
Technician	Tucker	Wife
Ted	Ty Grant	Wisteria Lane
Teen	Tyler	Neighbor
Teenage Boy	Umberto	Wisteria Lane
Teenager	Umpire	Neighborhood
Teller	Undercover Cop	Collie

Wisteria	Woman in Truck	Young Guy
Neighbor	Woman on Date	Young Man
Woman	Worker	Young Teacher
Woman #1	Workman	Young Tim
Woman #2	Xiao-Mei	Young Woman
Woman at Ballgame	Yaniv	Youth Camp Security
	Yao Lin	
Woman in Mattress Store	Young Bride-To-Be	Yuppie Woman
		Zach Young
Woman in Prison	Young Girl	Zach's Lawyer

Desperate Housewives Referenced In

- #LionelNationusImmersive Live Stream: The Postprandial Review of Hollywood's Self-Obsession (2019)
- ...So Goes the Nation (2006)
- 11th Annual Screen Actors Guild Awards (2005)
- 20 to 1: TV's Funniest Neighbours (2011)
- 2020 Republican National Convention: Night 1: Land of Promises (2020)
- 30 Rock: The Head and the Hair (2007)
- 500 Days of Summer (2009)
- America in Primetime: Independent Woman (2011)
- American Dad!
    - Not Particularly Desperate Housewife (2005)
    - The Last Ride of the Dodge City Rambler (2020)
- AniMat's Crazy Cartoon Cast: Shaq the Cartoon Cheapskate (2019)
- Arrested Development
    - Out on a Limb (2005)
    - Righteous Brothers (2005)
- Barry: Past = Present x Future Over Yesterday (2019)
- Beauty and the Geek: The Fixer-Uppers (2008)
- Behind the Truth (2013)
- Blood Father (2016)
- Body of Proof: Love Thy Neighbor (2011)
- Bones: The Truth in the Lye (2006)
- Breakfast: 14 June 2011 (2011)
- Bring It On: All or Nothing (2006)
- Brooklyn Nine-Nine: Serve & Protect (2017)
- Castle: One Man's Treasure (2009)
- Celebrity Wheel of Fortune

- - o Drew Carey, Teri Hatcher and Chrissy Metz (2021)
    - o Marcia Cross, Karl-Anthony Towns & Anthony Anderson (2022)
- Charmed: Desperate Housewitches (2005)
- Chelsea Lately: #6.43 (2012)
- Chris Rock: Kill the Messenger - London, New York, Johannesburg (2008)
- Close to Home: Suburban Prostitution (2005)
- Come Dine with Me: Basingstoke: Gill (2010)
- Community
    - o Advanced Introduction to Finality (2013)
    - o Social Psychology (2009)
- Consuming Passion (2008)
- Dancing with the Stars
    - o #11.5 (2011)
    - o Round Six (2009)
- Date Movie (2006)
- Dave's Old Porn: Kathy Griffin/Tom Byron (2012)
- De slimste mens ter wereld: #14.8 (2019)
- Dear Santa (2011) (TV Movie)
- Desperadas (2007)
- Desperate Houseboys (2005)
- Desperate Househusbands (2005)
- Desperate Housewhores 4 (2006)
- Desperate Housewives: Oprah Winfrey Is the New Neighbor (2005)
- Desperate Housewives: The Game (2006)
- Die Mitte der Welt (2016)
- Die schlechtesten Filme aller Zeiten
    - o Angel's Höllenkommando (2021)
    - o Hausfrauen-Report 3 (2019)
- Diminishing Returns
    - o American Beauty (2018)
    - o God's Not Dead (2018)
    - o Iron Man (2016)

- Down the Drain (2006)
- Drop Dead Diva: Desperate Housewife (2014)
- E! True Hollywood Story: The Women of Desperate Housewives (2005)
- EWTN Presents Bookmark: Crossing the Goal: Playbook on Our Father (2010)
- Entertainment Weekly's the New Classics: TV (2008)
- Entourage
    - Pie (2008)
    - Strange Days (2006)
- Evening Urgent: Eva Longoria/Elena Temnikova (2016)
- Everwood: Unspoken Truths (2004)
- Face Off: Death Becomes Them (2015)
- Faithful Word Baptist Church: Poem About TV Shows by Steven L. Anderson (2007)
- Family Guy
    - Baby Not on Board (2008)
    - The Father, the Son and the Holy Fonz (2005)
- Friends with Money (2006)
- Futurama: Neutopia (2011)
- Gavin & Stacey: #2.6 (2008)
- Gilmore Girls: The Prodigal Daughter Returns (2005)
- Glee: Acafellas (2009)
- Gravity Falls: Scary-oke (2014)
- Great TV Mistakes (2010) (TV Movie)
- Greek: The Wish-Pretzel (2009)
- Happy (2012)
- Harmontown: Joe Jackson: Steppin' Out (2013)
- Hitler's Place in History: The Faking of Adolf Hitler for History (2005)
- Hollywood Game Night: Super Duper Store Night (2017)
- How TV Changed Britain: Women (2008)
- I Could Never Be Your Woman (2007)
- I'm a Celebrity... Extra Camp: #4.12 (2019)

- It's a Dad, Dad, Dad, Dad World (2005)
- Jeopardy!
  - 2008 College Championship Final Game 2 (2008)
  - #22.102 (2006)
  - #22.203 (2006)
  - #26.76 (2009)
  - #26.78 (2009)
  - #26.93 (2010)
  - Million Dollar Celebrity Invitational Quarterfinal 1 (2009)
  - Million Dollar Celebrity Invitational Quarterfinal 5 (2010)
  - Million Dollar Celebrity Invitational Quarterfinal 6 (2010)
- Joey: Joey and the Beard (2006)
- Kickin' It: Wax on Wax off (2011)
- Knots Landing Reunion: Together Again (2005)
- La noche desesperada (2007)
- Late Night with Seth Meyers
  - Eva Longoria/Jason Mantzoukas/Sunil Yapa/Glenn Kotche (2016)
  - Eva Longoria/Max Greenfield/John Singleton/Venzella Joy (2017)
- Late Show with David Letterman
  - #12.136 (2005)
  - #17.15 (2009)
  - #17.70 (2010)
- Lemon Tree (2008)
- Life Unexpected: Plumber Cracked (2010)
- Living Will... (2010)
- Lost Girl: Adventures in Fae-bysitting (2013)
- Lost: The Final Season - Beginning of the End (2010)
- Love: One Long Day (2016)
- MADtv: #12.19 (2007)
- MADtv: Nicole Sullivan/Debra Wilson (2005)

- Make or Break TV: EZ Streets (2008)
- Mike and Mike in the Morning
    - 14 October 2016 (2016)
    - 24 July 2014 (2014)
- Minty Comedic Arts
    - 10 Things You Didn't Know About The Burbs (2020)
    - 10 Things You Didn't Know About Tremors (2021)
- More One Life to Live: #1.8 (2013)
- Most Extreme Elimination Challenge: Desperate Housewives vs. Ultimate Fighters (2005)
- MsMojo
    - Top 10 Forbidden TV Romances (2018)
    - Top 10 Funniest Going Into Labor Scenes in TV (2017)
    - Top 10 Greatest Primetime Soap Operas (2018)
    - Top 10 Heartbreaking Scenes in TV Dramas (2016)
    - Top 10 TV BFFs Who Hated Each Other in Real Life (2019)
    - Top 10 TV Couples with Ridiculous Age Gaps (2018)
    - Top 10 TV Series with All Female Leads (2017)
    - Top 10 Villainous TV Couples (2020)
    - Top 10 Worst TV Husbands (2016)
- My Fake Fiancé (2009) (TV Movie)
- NCIS: Naval Criminal Investigative Service: Road Kill (2008)
- NCIS: New Orleans: Desperate Navy Wives (2019)
- News at Ten: 13 September 2019 (2019)
- Nothing Like the Holidays (2008)
- Panique au ministère (2009) (TV Movie)
- Parks and Recreation: Pawnee Zoo (2009)

- Penn & Teller: Bullshit!: Gun Control (2005)
- Planet Sheen: Desperate Houseguests/Nesvidanya (2011)
- Portlandia: Inside Portlandia (2016)
- Private Traps: V síti (2011)
- Psych: Last Night Gus (2011)
- RTL Boulevard
    - #11.68 (2010)
    - #11.69 (2010)
    - #11.70 (2010)
- Ramy: Bay'ah (2020)
- RuPaul's Drag Race: RuPaul's Hair Extravaganza (2011)
- Sanctuary; Quite a Conundrum (2012)
- Saturday Night Live
    - Alec Baldwin/Christina Aguilera (2006)
    - Cameron Diaz/Green Day (2005)
    - Eva Longoria/Korn (2005)
    - Jake Gyllenhaal/The Shins (2007)
    - Jason Lee/Foo Fighters (2005)
    - Luke Wilson/U2 (2004)
    - Paris Hilton/Keane (2005)
    - Paul Giamatti/Ludacris featuring Sum-41 (2005)
    - Presidential Bash 2004 (2004) (TV Special)
    - Rainn Wilson/Arcade Fire (2007)
    - Tom Brady/Beck (2005)
- Screenwipe
    - #2.1 (2006)
    - #3.3 (2007)
    - Screenwipe USA (2006)
- Scrubs: My Big Bird (2006)
- Sexy Seductive Housewives (2010)
- Skins: Thomas (2009)
- Spaceballs: The Animated Series: Revenge of the Sithee (2008)

- Special Victims Unit: Ghost (2005)
- Spring Break Shark Attack (2005)
- St. Trinian's (2007)
- Studio 60 on the Sunset Strip: Pilot (2006)
- Supernatural: Slash Fiction (2011)
- Svengoolie: The Brides of Dracula (2006)
- Séries express
    - #2.39 (2009)
    - #2.42 (2009)
- TV Land Confidential: Oddballs & Original Characters (2007)
- TV: The Movie (2006)
- Taxaquizzen: #1.4 (2011)
- The 2000s: The Platinum Age Of Television (2018)
- The 57th Annual Primetime Emmy Awards (2005)
- The 58th Annual Primetime Emmy Awards (2006)
- The 59th Annual Primetime Emmy Awards (2007)
- The 61st Primetime Emmy Awards (2009)
- The 62nd Annual Golden Globe Awards 2005 (2005)
- The 63rd Annual Golden Globe Awards 2006 (2006)
- The 64th Annual Golden Globe Awards (2007)
- The Act: La Maison du Bon Reve (2019)
- The Amazing Race: Go, Mommy, Go! We Can Beat Them! (2005)
- The Arrivals (2008)
- The Cinema Snob: Trick or Treat (2016)
- The Comeback
    - Valerie Is Taken Seriously (2014)
    - Valerie Stands Out on the Red Carpet (2005)
- The Darkest Timeline with Ken Jeong & Joel McHale: Fake Endings with Daniel Dae Kim (2020)
- The Foursome (2006)
- The Graham Norton Show: #7.1 (2010)
- The Jay Leno Show: #1.67 (2009)
- The Knights of Prosperity: Operation: Oswald Montecristo (2007)

- The Muppets.: The Ex-Factor (2015)
- The New Adventures of Old Christine
    - Love Means Never Having to Say You're Crazy (2009)
    - Teach Your Children Well (2006)
- The Newsroom
    - 5/1 (2012)
    - I'll Try to Fix You (2012)
- The Nostalgia Critic: Foodfight! (2014)
- The O'Reilly Factor: 13 May 2008 (2008)
- The O.C.: The My Two Dads (2007)
- The Office: Michael's Birthday (2006)
- The Oprah Winfrey Show: 3 February 2005 (2005)
- The Other Woman (2014)
- The Real Housewives of Orange County: Dirty Housewives (2012)
- The Secret (2007)
- The Simpsons: Treehouse of Horror XVII (2006)
- The Story of Soaps (2020)
- The TV Set (2006)
- The Tonight Show Starring Jimmy Fallon
    - Jeremy Renner/Edie Falco/Tori Kelly (2015)
    - Michelle Pfeiffer/Kyle MacLachlan/Mark Normand (2017)
- The Tonight Show with Conan O'Brien
    - Brandon McMillan/Kerry Washington/Wilco (2009)
    - Howie Mandel/Alanis Morissette/Death Cab for Cutie (2009)
    - Will Ferrell/Pearl Jam (2009)
- The Tonight Show with Jay Leno
    - #19.136 (2011)
    - #19.159 (2011)
    - #19.20 (2010)
    - #19.206 (2011)
    - #21.20 (2012)

- - o Eva Longoria/Terry Crews/Cavalia's Odysseo (2013)
- The Unauthorized Melrose Place Story (2015)
- The Wright Stuff
    - o #13.40 (2010)
    - o #14.55 (2010)
    - o #17.161 (2012)
    - o #20.97 (2015)
- There Goes the Neighborhood: The Making of 'The 'Burbs' (2014)
- To kokkino domatio: ...Ki ola ta idia menoun... (2007)
- Todd's Pop Song Reviews: The Top Ten Worst Hit Songs of 2004 (2012)
- Touche pas à mon poste!: 29 October 2021 (2021)
- Tripping the Rift: The Movie (2008)
- Tripping the Rift: Witness Protection (2007)
- Tropic Thunder: Rain of Madness (2008)
- Trouble with the Curve (2012)
- TruInside: Heathers (2016)
- Tucker Carlson Tonight: 13 March 2019 (2019)
- Vecinos: La vampira bonita (2005)
- WatchMojo
    - o Top 10 Modern TV Shows That Jumped the Shark (2018)
    - o Top 10 Shows Men Secretly Like (2015)
    - o Top 10 Shows That Lost Their Mojo (2014)
    - o Top 10 TV Femme Fetales (2016)
    - o Top 10 TV MILFS (2014)
    - o Top 10 TV Shows That Lost Steam After a Great First Season (2016)
    - o Top 10 TV Wives Who Are the Absolute Worst (2016)
    - o Top 10 Worst TV Cast Feuds (2018)
- What I Like About You: Desperate Girlfriends (2006)
- Who Do You Think You Are?: Vanessa Williams (2011)

- Who Wants to Be a Millionaire: #7.154 (2009)
    - #7.85 (2009)
    - #8.160 (2010)
    - #8.29 (2009)
    - #8.71 (2009)
    - Teacher Week 5 (2008)
    - The Real Housewives of Millionaire 2 (2010)
- Whose Line Is It Anyway?: Jonathan Mangum 9 (2021)
- Will & Grace
    - From Queer to Eternity (2005)
    - Queens for a Day: Part 1 (2004)

Themed Episode Lists

Deaths
Mary Alice (1.1)
Martha Huber (1.8)
Karen's Son (1.14)
Juanita Solis (1.17)
Rex Van de Kamp (1.23)
Deidre Taylor (1.23, 8.2)
George Williams (2.9)
Curtis Monroe (2.11)
Susan's Grandmother (2.22)
Melanie Foster (2.23)
Ralph (2.23)
Noah Taylor (2.23)
Matthew Applewhite (2.24)
Carolyn Bigsby (3.7)
Nora Huntington (3.8)
Rebecca Shepherd (3.10)
Jane Hainsworth (3.13)
Monique Polier (3.15)
Edwin Hodge (3.15)
Alma Hodge (3.15)
Gilbert McCuskey (3.18)
Ilene Britt (3.23)
Lillian Simms (4.4)
Scruffles (4.6)
Victor Lang (4.9)
Ida Greenberg (4.10)
Sylvia Green (4.10)
Al Kaminsky (4.10)
Maynard Delfino (4.16)
Wayne Davis (4.17)
Ellie Leonard (4.17)
Dylan Davis (4.17)

Lila Dash (5.1, 5.24)
Paige Dash (5.1, 5.24)
Samuel Heller (5.8)
Glenn Wingfield (5.12)
Eli Scruggs (5.13)
Bradley Scott (5.16)
Edie Britt (5..18, 5.19, 5.20)
Daphne Bicks (6.10)
Jeff Bicks (6.10)
Emily Portsmith (6.8, 6.9)
Orson Hodge (6.11)
Karl Meyer (6.11)
Mona Clarke (6.11)
Patrick Scavo (6.11)
Iris Beckley (6.18)
Irina Korsakov (6.19)
Ramona (6.20)
Barbara Orlofsky (6.20)
Aunt Regina (6.21)
Patrick Logan (6.23)
Teresa Pruiit (6.23)
Frank Kaminski (7.14)
Beth Young (7.16)
Dick Barrows (7.18)
Felicia Tilman (7.22)
Cupcake (7.23)
Alejandro Perez/Ramon Sanchez (7.23)
Chuck Vance (8.9)
Orson Hodge (8.15)
Mike Delfino (8.16)
Karen McCluskey (8.23)

Births
Deanna Pruse Son (2.17)
Lily Solis/Helm (2.18)
Penny Scavo (2.24)

Gottlieb (4.6)
Benjamin/Simcha Hodge (4.6)
Maynard (MJ) Delfino (4.15, 5.1)
Paige Dash (5.1)
Polly Scavo (6.23)
Sophie Scavo (8.23)

Birthday Episodes
Julie Mayer (1.11)
Hazel (1.14)
Zach Young (1.15)
Topher Brennan (1.16)
Susan (2.12)
Danielle Van de Kamp (2.17, 2.22, 4.5)
Parker Scavo (3.1)
Gaby (3.14)
Travers (3.20)
Edie (4.2)
Emma's Princess Party (5.1)
Karen McCluskey (5.5)
Celia Solis (5.7)
Brandy (5.19)
Danny Bolen (6.4)
Juanita Solis (6.5, 7.11)
Brandon (6.9)
Penny Scavo (6.16)
Angie's Mother (6.6)
Renee Perry (7.9, 7.17)
Tom Scavo (8.19)

Christmas Episodes
1.5
3.8
3.10
6.10

6.11
8.7

Valentine's Day
1.14
2.15
8.13

Halloween
4.6
5.22
7.6
8.6

Mother's Day
4.15

Baby Shower
4.4

Disasters
Supermarket (3.7)
Tornado (4.9)
Car Crash (5.1, 5.24)
Fire at The White Horse (5.8)
Dave taking Susan and MJ hostage (5.24)
Julie attacked (6.2)
Plane crash (6.10)
Bomb (6.23)

Oktoberfest
6.5

Thanksgiving

6.15
7.8

Awards and Nominations

Won

- ADG Excellence in Production Design Awards, Single-Camera Television Series, 2005
- AFI Awards, TV Program of the Year, 2005
- ALMA Awards, Outstanding Television Series, 2011
- Bambi Awards, TV Series International, 2007
- Banff Television Festival
    - Best Continuing Series, 2005
- BMI Film & TV Awards
    - BMI TV Music Award, 2005
    - BMI TV Music Award, 2008
    - BMI TV Music Award, 2009
- Primetime Emmy Awards
    - Outstanding Lead Actress in a Comedy Series, 2005
    - Outstanding Casting for a Comedy Series, 2005
    - Outstanding Directing for a Comedy Series, 2005
    - Outstanding Guest Actress in a Comedy Series, 2005, 2008, 2010
    - Outstanding Main Title Theme Music, 2005
    - Outstanding Single-Camera Picture Editing for a Comedy Series, 2005
- GLAAD Media Awards
    - Outstanding Comedy Series, 2009
- Gold Derby Awards
    - Best Comedy Guest Actress, 2005, 2007
    - Best Comedy Episode of the Year, 2005, 2007
    - Breakthrough Performer of the Year, 2005

- o Best Comedy Actress, 2006
- o Performer of the Year, 2006
- o Best Comedy Guest Actor, 2009
- Golden Globe Awards
  - o Best Series - Musical or Comedy, 2005, 2006
  - o Best Actress Television - Series Musical or Comedy, 2005
- Golden Nymph Awards
  - o International TV Audience Award for Comedy TV Series, 2006, 2007, 2008, 2009, 2010, 2011, 2012
- NAACP Image Awards
  - o Outstanding Actress in a Comedy Series, 2012, 2013
- New York International Film and TV Festival
  - o Best Drama Series, 2009
- OFTA Television Awards
  - o Best Comedy Series, 2004
  - o Best Actress in a Comedy Series, 2004
  - o Best Lighting in a Series, 2004
  - o Best Production Design in a Series, 2004
  - o Best New Theme Song in a Series, Motion Picture or Miniseries, 2004
  - o Best New Title Sequence in a Series, Motion Picture or Miniseries, 2004
- People's Choice Awards
  - o Favorite New TV Drama, 2005
  - o Favorite Female TV Star, 2007
- PRISM Awards
  - o TV Comedy Series Multi-Episode Storyline, 2005
  - o Performance in a Comedy Series, 2008, 2009
- Publicists Guild of America
  - o Maxwell Weinberg Award for Television, 2005
- Satellite Awards

- - Best Television Series - Musical or Comedy, 2005
  - Best Actress - Musical or Comedy Series, 2005, 2006
  - Best Supporting Actress - Series, Miniseries or Television Film, 2011
- Screen Actors Guild Awards
  - Outstanding Performance by a Female Actor in a Comedy Series, 2005, 2006
  - Outstanding Performance by an Ensemble in a Comedy Series, 2005, 2006
- TCA Awards
  - Program of the Year, 2005
- Teen Choice Awards
  - Choice TV: Breakout Show, 2005
  - Choice V-Cast, 2005
  - Choice TV: Breakout Actor, 2005
  - Choice TV: Breakout Actress, 2005
  - Choice TV Actor: Comedy, 2006
- TP de Oro
  - Best Foreign Series, 2006
- TV Land Awards
  - Future Classic Award, 2005
- TV Quick and Choice Awards
  - Best New Drama. 2005
  - Best International TV Show, 2007
- Young Artist Awards
  - Best Young Actor Age Ten or Younger in a Comedy or Drama TV Series, 2005

Nominated

- ADG Excellence in Production Design Awards, 2006
- ALMA Awards

- o Outstanding Director of a Television Series, 2008
- o Outstanding Supporting Actor in a Drama Television Series, 2008
- o Outstanding Actor in a Comedy Series, 2009
- o Outstanding Actress in a Comedy Series, 2009
- o Favorite TV Actor – Leading Role, 2011
- American Cinema Editors, Best Edited One-Hour Series for Television, 2005
- Bafta Awards, Pioneer Audience Awards, 2006
- Banff Television Festival
  - o Best Comedy Program, 2006
  - o Best Comedy Program, 2008
  - o Best Continuing Series, 2009
- BET Awards
  - o Best Actress, 2006
- Casting Society of America
  - o Best Comedic Episodic Casting, 2005
  - o Best Comedic Episodic Casting, 2006
  - o Best Comedic Episodic Casting, 2007
- Cinema Audio Society Awards
  - o Outstanding Achievement in Sound Mixing for Television Series, 2010
- Costume Designers Guild Awards
  - o Best Costume Design - Contemporary TV Series, 2005
  - o Best Costume Design - Contemporary TV Series, 2006
  - o Best Costume Design - Contemporary TV Series, 2007
- Directors Guild of America Awards
  - o Outstanding Directing - Comedy Series, 2004
  - o Outstanding Directing - Comedy Series, 2007
- Primetime Emmy Awards
  - o Outstanding Comedy Series, 2005

- Outstanding Lead Actress in a Comedy Series, 2005, 2007
- Outstanding Art Direction for a Single-Camera Series, 2005, 2006
- Outstanding Costumes for a Series, 2005, 2006, 2007, 2008
- Outstanding Guest Actress in a Comedy Series, 2005, 2006, 2007, 2008
- Outstanding Main Title Design, 2005
- Outstanding Single-Camera Picture Editing for a Comedy Series, 2005, 2006
- Outstanding Writing for a Comedy Series, 2005
- Outstanding Supporting Actress in a Comedy Series, 2006
- Outstanding Hairstyling for a Series, 2006, 2007
- Outstanding Casting for a Comedy Series, 2006, 2007
- Outstanding Hairstyling for a Single-Camera Series, 2008, 2009
- Outstanding Guest Actor in a Comedy Series, 2009
- Outstanding Voice-Over Performance, 2011, 2012
- GLAAD Media Awards
  - Outstanding Comedy Series, 2007, 2008
- Gold Derby Awards
  - Best Comedy Series, 2005, 2006, 2007, 2008, 2012
  - Best Comedy Actress, 2005, 2006, 2007, 2008, 2009, 2012
  - Best Comedy Supporting Actress, 2005, 2007, 2008
  - Best Comedy Guest Actress, 2005, 2006
  - Best Comedy Guest Actor, 2005
  - Best Comedy Episode of the Year, 2005, 2006, 2008, 2009

- o Performer of the Year, 2005
- o Breakthrough Performer of the Year, 2005
- o Best Ensemble of the Year, 2006
- Golden Globe Awards
  - o Best Actress Television - Series Musical or Comedy, 2005, 2006, 2007
  - o Best Supporting Actress - Series, Miniseries, or TV Film, 2005
- Goldene Kamera
  - o Best US Series, 2009
- IFMCA Awards
  - o Best Original Score for Television, 2004
- Imagen Foundation Awards
  - o Best Television Actress, 2005, 2007
  - o Best Television Actor, 2010
- Golden Reel Awards
  - o Best Sound Editing in Television Episodic - Music, 2005
  - o Best Sound Editing in Television Short Form - Music, 2005
- NAACP Image Awards
  - o Outstanding Supporting Actor in a Comedy Series, 2006
  - o Outstanding Actress in a Comedy Series, 2012
- National Television Awards
  - o Most Popular Drama, 2005, 2006, 2008
  - o Outstanding Drama Performance, 2008
- OFTA Television Awards
  - o Best Actress in a Comedy Series, 2004, 2005, 2006, 2007
  - o Best Guest Actress in a Comedy Series, 2004, 2005, 2006, 2007
  - o Best Ensemble in a Comedy Series, 2004, 2005, 2006, 2007
  - o Best Direction in a Comedy Series, 2004, 2007

- - o Best Writing in a Comedy Series, 2004, 2005, 2007
    - o Best Music in a Series, 2004
    - o Best Costume Design in a Series, 2004, 2008
    - o Best Makeup/Hairstyling in a Series, 2004
    - o Best Sound in a Series, 2004
    - o Best Comedy Series, 2005
- People's Choice Awards
  - o Favorite TV Drama, 2006
  - o Favorite Female TV Star, 2006
  - o Favorite TV Comedy Actress, 2010
  - o Favorite TV Family, 2011
  - o Favorite TV Actress, 2012
- PRISM Awards
  - o TV Comedy Series Episode, 2005, 2011
  - o Performance in a Comedy Series, 2005, 2007, 2008, 2009, 2012
- Producers Guild of America Awards
  - o Outstanding Producer of Episodic Television - Comedy Series, 2006
- Satellite Awards
  - o Best Actress - Musical or Comedy Series, 2005, 2006, 2007
  - o Best Supporting Actress - Series, Miniseries or Television Film, 2006, 2007, 2011
  - o Best DVD Release - Television Series, 2005
- Screen Actors Guild Awards
  - o Outstanding Performance by a Female Actor in a Comedy Series, 2007
  - o Outstanding Performance by an Ensemble in a Comedy Series, 2007, 2008, 2009
- TCA Awards
  - o Outstanding Achievement in Comedy, 2005
  - o Outstanding New Program, 2005
  - o Individual Achievement in Comedy, 2005
- Teen Choice Awards

- o Choice TV Show: Comedy, 2005, 2006, 2007, 2008, 2009
- o Choice TV Actor: Comedy, 2005, 2006
- o Choice TV Actress: Comedy, 2005, 2006, 2007, 2008
- TP de Oro
  - o Best Foreign Series, 2008, 2010
- Writers Guild of America Awards
  - o Best Writing in Television - Episodic Comedy, 2005, 2006
- Women's Image Network Awards
  - o Actress in Drama Series, 2005
- Young Artist Awards
  - o Best Leading Young Actress in a Comedy or Drama TV Series, 2005
  - o Best Supporting Young Actor in a Comedy or Drama TV Series, 2005
  - o Best Young Recurring Actress on a Comedy Series, 2006, 2007
  - o Best Performance in a TV Series (Comedy or Drama) - Guest Starring Young Actress, 2007
  - o Best Young Recurring Actress in a Comedy Series, 2008
  - o Best Young Recurring Actor in a Comedy Series, 2008

Desperate Housewives by the Numbers

Episodes: 180
Dinner parties: 6
Secrets: 729
Advertising Accounts: 17
Marriages: 19
Break Ups: 88
Divorces: 6
Pregnancies: 20
Affairs: 23
Television Shows: 21
Murders: 21
Illnesses: 136
Businesses: 500
Musicals: 16
Events: 173
Deaths: 63
Births: 9
Birthdays: 21
Disasters: 8
Movies: 65

NOISY FULFILLMENT
A REFERENCE GUIDE

Love and Relationships in Desperate Housewives

One of the major themes throughout the show, is how the 'housewives' navigate themselves through their romantic relationships, and how these relationships often set the scene for a lot of what goes on in the *Desperate Housewives* universe. From the love-conquers-all romance of Mike and Susan spanning eight seasons, to the dark, ominous relationships such as Bree and George, and Danielle and Matthew, *Desperate Housewives* explored a spectrum of different pairings, all of which served the plot in some crucial way.

But it wasn't all roses (or wisteria). For such a beautiful, idyllic suburb, Wisteria Lane saw a lot of complicated relationships. Throughout eight seasons, we became third wheels to the relationships on the lane and watched as the wives dealt with adultery, secrets, parenting, financial problems, break-ups, and even spousal deaths. We watched relationships like Bree and Trip's evolve from lawyer-client to husband and wife, and rooted for Carlos and Gaby, and Mike and Susan to work things out…again. According to Lazzarus, "the main characters living on Wisteria Lane also pursue **relationships** and prioritize love in their lives over nearly everything else."

This section contains a guide to all of the love interests in the show – documenting first dates, engagements, affairs, weddings, and more. It also contains a catalogue of relationship 'lists', which allow you to follow any one relationship from start to finish, by watching all of the episodes in the order they are listed. So, go forth, and let yourself get swept away by one of the Desperate Housewives romances.

"Love can bring out the best in us…the confidence to move on, the courage to tell the truth, the strength to keep hoping"

- Mary Alice Young

Relationships

Lynette Lindquist/Scavo

Tom Scavo (1.1, 1.2, 1.3, 1.4, 1.5, 1.7, 1.9, 1.11, 1.14, 1.15, 1.17, 1.20, 1.21, 1.22, 2.11, 2.12, 2.13, 2.14, 2.15, 2.16, 2.17, 2.20, 2.21, 2.22, 2.23, 2.24, 3.1, 3.2, 3.3, 3.4, 3.5, 3.6, 3.7, 3.8, 3.9, 3.10, 3.11, 3.12, 3.13, 3.15, 3.16, 3.18, 3.19, 3.20, 3.21, 3.22, 4.1, 4.3, 4.4, 4.5, 4.6, 4.7, 4.8, 4.9, 4.12, 4.13, 4.14, 4.15, 4.16, 4.17, 5.1, 5.2, 5.3, 5.4, 5.5, 5.6, 5.7, 5.8, 5.9, 5.10, 5.11, 5.12, 5.13, 5.14, 5.15, 5.16, 5.17, 5.18, 5.20, 5.21, 5.22, 5.23, 5,24, 6.1, 6.2, 6.3, 6.4, 6.5, 6.6, 6.7, 6.8, 6.9, 6.10, 6.11, 6.12, 6.13, 6.14, 6.15, 6.16, 6.17, 6.18, 6.19, 6.20, 6.21, 6.22, 6.23, 7.1, 7.2, 7.3, 7.5, 7.6, 7.7, 7.8, 7.9, 7.10, 7.11, 7.12, 7.13, 7.14, 7.16, 7.17, 7.18, 7.19, 7.20, 7.21, 7.22, 7.23, 8.1, 8.2, 8.3, 8.4, 8.5, 8.6, 8.7, 8.8, 8.9, 8.10, 8,12, 8.13, 8.14, 8.15, 8.16, 8.17, 8.18, 8.19, 8.20, 8.21, 8.22, 8.23)
Carlos Solis (2.11)
Chuck (2.5)
Rick Coletti (3.18, 3.19, 3.20, 3.21, 3.22, 3.23, 4.12, 4.13)
First Boyfriend (5.2)
Two of the guys from the Rugby team (7.1)
Phil (8.5)
Preston's friend (8.5)
Guy with tie and remote (8.5)
Scott (8.5)
Roberta in accounting (6.8)
Frank (8.12, 8.13)
Greg (8.20, 8.21)

Bree Mason/Van De Kamp/Hodge/Weston

Rex Van de Kamp (1.1, 1.2, 1.3, 1.4, 1.5, 1.6, 1.7, 1.8, 1.9, 1.10, 1.11, 1.13, 1.14, 1.15, 1.16, 1.17, 1.18, 1.19, 1.20, 1.21, 2.2, 2.3, 2.5, 2.6, 2.8, 2.9, 2.12, 2.15, 2.23, 2.24, 3.4, 3.16, 4.4, 4.8, 5.2, 5.9, 5.11, 5.13, 6.17, 6.18, 6.21, 7.1, 7.18, 7.19, 8.17)
Tai Grant (1.2, 2.8)
Unnamed Boyfriend (1.8)
George Williams (1.11, 1.12, 1.13, 1.20, 1.21, 1.22, 2.3, 2.4, 2.5, 2.6, 2.8, 2.9, 2.10, 2.24, 7.21)
Peter McMillan (2.17, 2.18, 2.19, 2.20, 2.21)
Orson Hodge (2.23, 2.24, 3.1, 3.2, 3.3, 3.4, 3.5, 3.6, 3.7, 3.8, 3.9, 3.10, 3.11, 3.12, 3.13, 3.14, 3.15, 3.16, 3.23, 4.1, 4.2, 4.3, 4.4, 4.5, 4.6, 4.7, 4.8, 4.9, 4.10, 4.11, 4.12, 4.13, 4.14, 4.15, 4.16, 4.17, 5.1, 5.2, 5.3, 5.4, 5.5, 5.6, 5.7, 5.8, 5.9, 5.10, 5.11, 5.12, 5.15, 5.16, 5.17, 5.18, 5.19, 5.20, 5.21, 5.22, 5.23, 5.24, 6.1, 6.2, 6.3, 6.4, 6.5, 6.6, 6.7, 6.8, 6.9, 6.10, 6.11, 6.12, 6.13, 6.14, 6.15, 6.18, 6.19, 6.21, 6.22, 6.23, 7.1, 7.2, 7.6, 7.11, 7.19, 7.21, 8.2, 8.9, 8.13, 8.14, 8.15, 8.16, 8.19)
Reverend Green (4.16)
Karl Mayer (5.21, 5.22, 5.23, 5.24, 6.1, 6.2, 6.3, 6.4, 6.5, 6.6, 6.8, 6.9, 6.10, 6.11, 6.12, 6.14, 6.16, 7.19)
Keith Watson (7.1, 7.2, 7.3, 7.4, 7.5, 7.6, 7.7, 7.8, 7.9, 7.10, 7.11, 7.12, 7.13, 7.14, 7.15)
Richard Watson (7.8, 7.9, 7.10)
Bradley (8.11)
Guy at bar (8.11)
Man #1 (8.12)
Man #2 (8.12)
Man #3 (8.12)
Man #4 (8.12)
Man #5 (8.12)

Man #6 (8.12)
Man #7 (8.12)
Don (8.12)
Greg (8.12)
Man with a firm bicep (8.12)
Blonde Guy (8.13)
Man with blue truck (8.13)
Man with Dark Hair and sports car (8.13)
Guy with motorcycle (8.13)
Jerry (8.13)
Man (8.13)
Man at bar (8.13)
Chuck Vance (7.20, 7.21, 7.22, 7.23, 8.1, 8.2, 8.3, 8.4, 8.7, 8.8, 8.9, 8.10)
Trip Weston (8.19, 8.20, 8.21, 8.22, 8.23)

Gabrielle Marquez/Lang/Solis

Half the Yankee Outfield (1.1)
Carlos Solis (1.1, 1.2, 1.3, 1.4, 1.5, 1.6, 1.7, 1.8, 1.9,
1.10, 1.11, 1.13, 1.14, 1.15, 1.16, 1.17, 1.18, 1.19, 1.20,
1.21, 1.22, 2.1, 2.3, 2.4, 2.5, 2.6, 2.8, 2.9, 2.10, 2.11,
2.12, 2.13, 2.14, 2.15, 2.16, 2.17, 2.18, 2.19, 2.20, 2.21,
2.22, 2.23, 2.24, 3,2, 3.3, 3.4, 3.5, 3.6, 3.7, 3.9, 3.11,
3.12, 3.15, 3.16, 3.23, 4.1, 4.2, 4.3, 4.4, 4.5, 4.6, 4.7,
4.8, 4.9, 4.10, 4.11, 4.12, 4.13, 4.14, 4.15, 4.16, 4.17,
5.1, 5.2, 5.3, 5.4, 5.5, 5.6, 5.7, 5.8, 5.9, 5.10, 5.11, 5.12,
5.13, 5.14, 5.15, 5.16, 5.17, 5.18, 5.20, 5.21, 5.22, 5.23,
5.24, 6.1, 6.2, 6.3, 6.4, 6.5, 6.6, 6.7, 6.8, 6.9, 6.10, 6.11,
6.12, 6.14, 6.15, 6.16, 6.17, 6.18, 6.19, 6.20, 6.21, 6.22,
6.23, 7.1, 7.2, 7.3, 7.4, 7.5, 7.6, 7.7, 7.8, 7.9, 7.10, 7.11,
7.12, 7.13, 7.14, 7.15, 7.16, 7.18, 7.19, 7.20, 7.21, 7.23,
8.2, 8.3, 8.4, 8.5, 8.6, 8.7, 8.8, 8.9, 8.10, 8.11, 8.13,
8.14, 8.14, 8.16, 8.17, 8.18, 8.19, 8.20, 8.22, 8.23)
John Rowland (1.1, 1.2, 1.3, 1.4, 1.5, 1.6, 1.7, 1.8, 1.9,
1.13, 1.15, 1.18, 1.19, 1.20, 1.21, 1.22, 2.1, 2.3, 2.11,
2.16, 2.24, 3.3, 3.4, 3.13, 3.17, 4.3, 4.5, 5.16, 5.18, 5.20,
6.3, 6.4, 6.20, 719, 8.23)
Famous Fashion Photographer (1.9)
Scott (2.12)
Sam (1.19)
David Bradley (2.4, 2.5, 2.6)
Phil Lopez (3.5)
Jason (3.5, 8.19)
Bill Pearce (3.10, 3.11)
Zach Young (3.11, 3.12, 3.13, 3.14, 3.15)
Luke Purdue (3.14)
Toby (3.18)
Victor Lang (3.16, 3.17, 3.18, 3.19, 3.20, 3.21, 3.22,
3.23, 4.1, 4.3, 4.4, 4.5, 4.6, 4.7, 4.8, 4.9, 4.10)
Adam Mayfair (4.3)
Roy (4.16)

Twizzle Stick #17 (5.19)
Mick Jagger (7.14)
Frank Sweeney (8.8)
David Lee Roth (8.13)

Edie Britt/McClain/Rothwell/Williams

Handyman (1.1)
Tennis Coach (1.1)
Priest/Minister (1.1)
Unknown Date (1.1)
Mr. Rothwell (1.2)
Javier (1.2)
Mike Delfino (1.1, 1.2, 1.4, 3.3, 3.5, 3.6, 3.8, 3.9, 3.10)
Karl Mayer (1.11, 2.2, 2.3, 2.7, 2.11, 2.13, 2.14, 2.15, 2.18, 2.19, 2.20, 2.21)
Bill (1.17)
Cyrus (1.22)
Cable Guy (3.6)
Folk Singing Duo (3.6)
Rabbi Littman (3.6)
Carlos Solis (3.17, 3.18, 3.19, 3.20, 3.21, 3.22, 3.23, 4.1, 4.2, 4.3, 4.4, 4.5, 4.6, 4.9, 4.11, 4.13)
Charles McLain (3.16, 3.21, 5.19)
Man #1 (3.18)
Man #2 (3.18)
Man #3 (3.18)
Orson Hodge (4.14, 4.15)
David Dash/Williams (5.1, 5.2, 5.3, 5.4, 5.5, 5.6, 5.8, 5.9, 5.10, 5.11, 5.12, 5.13, 5.14, 5.15, 5.17, 5.18, 5.19, 5.20, 5.23)
Edie and Umberto (5.13)
Edie and Eli Scruggs (5.13)
Ed (5.19)

Susan Bremmer/Mayer/Delfino

Karl Mayer (1.1, 1.2, 1.3, 1.4, 1.5, 1.7, 1.9, 1.10, 1.11, 1.22, 1.23, 2.2, 2.3, 2.5, 2.7, 2.14, 2.15, 2.16, 2.17, 2.18, 2.19, 2.21, 2.22, 2.23, 2.24, 3.8, 3.17, 3.22, 4.14, 5.2, 5.8, 5.13, 5.18, 5.19, 5.21, 6.4, 6.6, 6.9, 6.11, 6.12, 6.19, 8.13)
Mike Delfino (1.1, 1.2, 1.3, 1.4, 1.5, 1.7, 1.8, 1.10, 1.11, 1.14, 1.15, 1.17, 1.18, 1.21, 1.22, 2.1, 2.4, 2.6, 2.7, 2.8, 2.14, 2.21, 2.22, 2.23, 2.24, 3.1, 3.2, 3.3, 3.4, 3.5, 3.8, 3.10, 3.11, 3.13, 3.16, 3.17, 3.18, 3.19, 3.20, 3.21, 3.22, 3.23, 4.1, 4.2, 4.4, 4.5, 4.6, 4.7, 4.8, 4.9, 4.10, 4.13, 4.14, 4.15, 4.16, 4.17, 5.1, 5.2, 5.3, 5.4, 5.8, 5.9, 5.10, 5.12, 5.13, 5.14, 5.15, 5.16, 5.20, 5.21, 5.22, 5.23, 5.24, 6.1, 6.2, 6.4, 6.5, 6.6, 6.7, 6.8, 6.9, 6.10, 6.11, 6.12, 6.13, 6.14, 6.15, 6.16, 6.17, 6.19, 6.20, 6.21, 6.22, 6.23, 7.1, 7.2, 7.3, 7.4, 7.5, 7.6, 7.8, 7.9, 7.10, 7.11, 7.12, 7.14, 7.16, 7.17, 7.19, 7.20, 7.22, 7.23, 8.1, 8.2, 8.3, 8.4, 8.7, 8.9, 8.10, 8.11, 8.12, 8.13, 8.14, 8.15, 8.16, 8.17, 8.18, 8.19, 8.23)
Officer Thompson (1.5)
Bill (1.17)
Lamont (1.19)
Lonnie Moon (2.5)
Jim Halverson (2.12)
Doctor Ron Mcready (2.12, 2.13, 2.15, 2.16, 2.17, 2.18, 5.12)
Gary Grantham (2.14)
Orson Hodge (2.19)
Gus (2.21)
Ian Hainsworth (3.1, 3.2, 3.3, 3.4, 3.6, 3.7, 3.8, 3.9, 3.10, 3.11, 3.13, 3.14, 3.15, 3.16, 3.17, 3.18, 3.19, 3.20, 3.21, 3.22)
Jackson Braddock (4.17, 5.1, 5.2, 5.4, 5.5, 5.6, 5.7, 5.8, 5.9, 5.10, 5.11, 5.12, 5.13, 5.21, 5.22, 5.23)
Lee McDermott (5.11)

Todd Shaffer (5.12)
Jessie (5.17)
Mark Malone (6.7)
It is also notes that Susan had seven boyfriends through hs and college (5.12)
Roy Bender (6.16)
Eddie Orlofsky (6.20)
Curtis Monroe (7.14)

Renee Perry/Faulkner

Doug Perry (7.1, 7.2, 7.5, 7.6, 7.15, 7.20, 7.23, 8.6, 8.11, 8.14, 8.18, 8.20)
French Guy on Ski Trip (7.2)
Keith Watson (7.3, 7.4)
Lawyer (7.5)
Tom Scavo (7.2, 7.8, 7.9, 7.10, 7.11, 7.12)
Guy at Restaurant (7.9)
Brian (7.16)
Dead Linebacker (7.21)
Ben Falkner (7.23, 8.2, 8.6, 8.9, 8.10, 8.11, 8.12, 8.14, 8.15, 8.18, 8.19, 8.20, 8.22, 8.23)
Shrink (8.10)

Katherine Mayfair/Davis

Adam Mayfair (4.1, 4.2, 4.3, 4.5, 4.6, 4.7, 4.9, 4.10, 4.11, 4.16, 4.17)
Wayne Davis (4.3, 4.7, 4.11, 4.12, 4.13, 4.14, 4.15, 4.16, 4.17)
Tim (4.11)
Mike Delfino (5.6, 5.7, 5.8, 5.9, 5.10, 5.12, 5.14, 5.15, 5.16, 5.17, 5.20, 5.21, 5.22, 5.23, 5.24, 6.1, 6.2, 6.4, 6.5, 6.6, 6.7, 6.8, 6.9, 6.10, 6.13)
Peter Hickey (5.6)
Robyn Gallagher (6.15, 6.16, 6.17, 6.18, 8.23)
David (6.18)

Mary Alice Young/Angela Forrest

Todd Forrest/Paul Young (1.1, 1.2, 1.3, 1.4, 1.8, 1.15, 2.15, 7.1, 7.4, 7.12, 7.15, 7.18, 7.22, 8.23)

Tom Scavo

Lynette Scavo (1.1, 1.2, 1.3, 1.4, 1.5, 1.7, 1.9, 1.11, 1.14, 1.15, 1.17, 1.20, 1.21, 1.22, 2.11, 2.12, 2.13, 2.14, 2.15, 2.16, 2.17, 2.20, 2.21, 2.22, 2.23, 2.24, 3.1, 3.2, 3.3, 3.4, 3.5, 3.6, 3.7, 3.8, 3.9, 3.10, 3.11, 3.12, 3.13, 3.15, 3.16, 3.18, 3.19, 3.20, 3.21, 3.22, 4.1, 4.3, 4.4, 4.5, 4.6, 4.7, 4.8, 4.9, 4.12, 4.13, 4.14, 4.15, 4.16, 4.17, 5.1, 5.2, 5.3, 5.4, 5.5, 5.6, 5.7, 5.8, 5.9, 5.10, 5.11, 5.12, 5.13, 5.14, 5.15, 5.16, 5.17, 5.18, 5.20, 5.21, 5.22, 5.23, 5,24, 6.1, 6.2, 6.3, 6.4, 6.5, 6.6, 6.7, 6.8, 6.9, 6.10, 6.11, 6.12, 6.13, 6.14, 6.15, 6.16, 6.17, 6.18, 6.19, 6.20, 6.21, 6.22, 6.23, 7.1, 7.2, 7.3, 7.5, 7.6, 7.7, 7.8, 7.9, 7.10, 7.11, 7.12, 7.13, 7.14, 7.16, 7.17, 7.18, 7.19, 7.20, 7.21, 7.22, 7.23, 8.1, 8.2, 8.3, 8.4, 8.5, 8.6, 8.7, 8.8, 8.9, 8.10, 8,12, 8.13, 8.14, 8.15, 8.16, 8.17, 8.18, 8.19, 8.20, 8.21, 8.22, 8.23)
Claire (1.11)
Anabel Foster (1.20, 1.21)
Nora Huntington (1.13, 2.22, 2.23, 2.24, 3.1, 3.5, 3.6, 3.7)
Patty Rizzo (5.20)
Jane Carlson (8.4, 8.5, 8.6, 8.7, 8.8, 8.9, 8.10, 8.12, 8.13, 8.15, 8.16, 8.17, 8.18, 8.19, 8.20, 8.21, 8.22)
Renee Perry (7.2, 7.8, 7.9, 7.10, 7.11, 7.12)

Carlos Solis

Gabrielle Marquez/Lang/Solis (1.1, 1.2, 1.3, 1.4, 1.5, 1.6, 1.7, 1.8, 1.9, 1.10, 1.11, 1.13, 1.14, 1.15, 1.16, 1.17, 1.18, 1.19, 1.20, 1.21, 1.22, 2.1, 2.3, 2.4, 2.5, 2.6, 2.8, 2.9, 2.10, 2.11, 2.12, 2.13, 2.14, 2.15, 2.16, 2.17, 2.18, 2.19, 2.20, 2.21, 2.22, 2.23, 2.24, 3,2, 3.3, 3.4, 3.5, 3.6, 3.7, 3.9, 3.11, 3.12, 3.15, 3.16, 3.23, 4.1, 4.2, 4.3, 4.4, 4.5, 4.6, 4.7, 4.8, 4.9, 4.10, 4.11, 4.12, 4.13, 4.14, 4.15, 4.16, 4.17, 5.1, 5.2, 5.3, 5.4, 5.5, 5.6, 5.7, 5.8, 5.9, 5.10, 5.11, 5.12, 5.13, 5.14, 5.15, 5.16, 5.17, 5.18, 5.20, 5.21, 5.22, 5.23, 5.24, 6.1, 6.2, 6.3, 6.4, 6.5, 6.6, 6.7, 6.8, 6.9, 6.10, 6.11, 6.12, 6.14, 6.15, 6.16, 6.17, 6.18, 6.19, 6.20, 6.21, 6.22, 6.23, 7.1, 7.2, 7.3, 7.4, 7.5, 7.6, 7.7, 7.8, 7.9, 7.10, 7.11, 7.12, 7.13, 7.14, 7.15, 7.16, 7.18, 7.19, 7.20, 7.21, 7.23, 8.2, 8.3, 8.4, 8.5, 8.6, 8.7, 8.8, 8.9, 8.10, 8.11, 8.13, 8.14, 8.16, 8.17, 8.18, 8.19, 8.20, 8.22, 8.23)
Lynette Scavo (2.11)
Xiao-Mei (2.21, 2.22, 2.23, 2.24, 3.1)
Nora Huntington (3.2)
Trishelle (3.5)
Date (3.11)
Edie Britt (3.17, 3.18, 3.19, 3.20, 3.21, 3.22, 3.23, 4.1, 4.2, 4.3, 4.4, 4.5, 4.6, 4.9, 4.11, 4.13)
Dancer (3.16)
Virginia Hildebrand (5.6)
Lucy Blackburn (5.17, 5.18, 5.20)
Susan (8.3)

Mike Delfino

Amy Delfino (1.2, 1.12, 6.11)
Susan Mayer / Delfino (1.1, 1.2, 1.3, 1.4, 1.5, 1.7, 1.8, 1.10, 1.11, 1.14, 1.15,1.17, 1.18, 1.21, 1.22, 2.1, 2.4, 2.6, 2.7, 2.8, 2.14, 2.21, 2.22, 2.23, 2.24, 3.1, 3.2, 3.3, 3.4, 3.5, 3.8, 3.10, 3.11, 3.13, 3.16, 3.17, 3.18, 3.19, 3.20, 3.21, 3.22, 3.23, 4.1, 4.2, 4.4, 4.5, 4.6, 4.7, 4.8, 4.9, 4.10, 4.13, 4.14, 4.15, 4.16, 4.17, 5.1, 5.2, 5.3, 5.4, 5.8, 5.9, 5.10, 5.12, 5.13, 5.14, 5.15, 5.16, 5.20, 5.21, 5.22, 5.23, 5.24, 6.1, 6.2, 6.4, 6.5, 6.6, 6.7, 6.8, 6.9, 6.10, 6.11, 6.12, 6.13, 6.14, 6.15, 6.16, 6.17, 6.19, 6.20, 6.21, 6.22, 6.23, 7.1, 7.2, 7.3, 7.4, 7.5, 7.6, 7.8, 7.9, 7.10, 7.11, 7.12, 7.14, 7.16, 7.17, 7.19, 7.20, 7.22, 7.23, 8.1, 8.2, 8.3, 8.4, 8.7, 8.9, 8.10, 8.11, 8.12, 8.13, 8.14, 8.15, 8.16, 8.17, 8.18, 8.19, 8.23)
Edie Britt (1.1, 1.2, 1.4, 3.3, 3.5, 3.6, 3.8, 3.9, 3.10)
Deirde Taylor (1.12, 1.19, 1.21, 1.22, 8.2)
Date at the movies (2.19)
Missy Taylor (4.2)
Date (5.6)
Katherine Mayfair (5.6, 5.7, 5.8, 5.9, 5.10, 5.12, 5.14, 5.15, 5.16, 5.17, 5.20, 5.21, 5.22, 5.23, 5.24, 6.1, 6.2, 6.4, 6.5, 6.6, 6.7, 6.8, 6.9, 6.10, 6.13)

Karl Mayer

Susan Bremmer/Mayer/Delfino (1.1, 1.2, 1.3, 1.4, 1.5, 1.7, 1.9, 1.10, 1.11, 1.22, 1.23, 2.2, 2.3, 2.5, 2.7, 2.14, 2.15, 2.16, 2.17, 2.18, 2.19, 2.21, 2.22, 2.23, 2.24, 3.8, 3.17, 3.22, 4.14, 5.2, 5.8, 5.13, 5.18, 5.19, 5.21, 6.4, 6.6, 6.9, 6.11, 6.12)
Brandi (1.3, 1.11, 5.13)
Redhead (5.13)
Edie Britt (1.11, 2.2, 2.3, 2.7, 2.11, 2.13, 2.14, 2.15, 2.18, 2.19, 2.20, 2.21)
Woman #1 (2.20)
Woman #2 (2.20)
Woman #3 (2.20)
Marisa Mayer (4.14, 5.18)
Susan's Cousin (4.14)
Bree Van de Kamp (5.21, 5.22, 5.23, 5.24, 6.1, 6.2, 6.3, 6.4, 6.5, 6.6, 6.8, 6.9, 6.10, 6.11, 6.12, 6.14, 6.16, 7.19)
Candice (6.3)
Brandy (6.11)
Amber the Dental Hygienist (6.11)
Kwan Lee (6.11)
The Cable Lady (6.11)
Karl and Courtney the Yoga Instructor (6.11)

Keith Watson

Renee Perry (7.3, 7.4)
Bree Van de Kamp (7.1, 7.2, 7.3, 7.4, 7.5, 7.6, 7.7, 7.8, 7.9, 7.10, 7.11, 7.12, 7.13, 7.14, 7.15)
Amber James (7.13, 7.14, 7.15)
Stephanie (7.3)

Doug Perry

Renee Perry (7.1, 7.2, 7.5, 7.6, 7.15, 7.20, 7.23, 8.6, 8.11, 8.14, 8.18, 8.20)
Doug and Agent's Assistant (7.1)

Sophie Bremmer/Flickman

Morty Flickman (1.18, 1.21, 2.6, 2.8, 2.9)
Man who liked to gamble (1.21)
Man who liked to drink (1.21)
Man who liked other men (1.21)
Hector (1.19)
Addison Prudy (2.8)

Paul Young/Todd Forrest

Mary Alice Young/Angela Forrest (1.1, 1.2, 1.3, 1.4, 1.8, 1.15, 2.15, 7.1, 7.4, 7.12, 7.15, 7.18, 7.22, 8.23)
Edie Britt (1.16)
Beth Young (7.2, 7.3, 7.4, 7.6, 7.7, 7.8, 7.10, 7.11, 7.12, 7.13, 7.15, 7.16, 7.17, 7.18, 7.19, 7.20, 7.22)

Greg

Lynette Scavo (8.20, 8.21)
Ex-wife (8.12)
Crystal (8.20)

Frank

Ex-wife (8.12)
Lynette (8.12, 8.13)

Porter Scavo

SarahJ/Lynette (5.2)
Anne Shilling (5.6, 5.7, 5.9, 5.10)
Julie Mayer (8.14)

Anne Shilling

Porter Scavo (5.6, 5.7, 5.9)
Warren Schilling (5.8, 5.9)

Preston Scavo

Irina (6.17, 6.18, 6.19, 6.22)

Nora Huntington

Tom Scavo 1.13, 2.22, 2.23, 2.24, 3.1, 3.5, 3.6, 3.7
Turk (3.2)
Carlos Solis (3.2)

Chuck Vance

Bree Van de Kamp/Hodge (7.20, 7.21, 7.22, 7.23, 8.1, 8.2, 8.3, 8.4, 8.7, 8.8, 8.9, 8.10, 8.15, 8.17, 8.21)
Doreen Vance (7.21, 7.23)

Rex Van De Kamp

Bree Van De Kamp (1.1, 1.2, 1.3, 1.4, 1.5, 1.6, 1.7, 1.8, 1.9, 1.10, 1.11, 1.13, 1.14, 1.15, 1.16, 1.17, 1.18, 1.19, 1.20, 1.21, 2.2, 2.3, 2.5, 2.6, 2.8, 2.9, 2.12, 2.15, 2.23, 2.24, 3.4, 3.16, 4.4, 4.8, 5.2, 5.9, 5.11, 5.13, 6.17, 6.18, 6.21, 7.1, 7.18, 7.19, 8.17)
Maisy Gibbons (1.10, 1.16)
Lillian (6.17, 6.18, 6.21)

Lucia Perez/Marquez

Charles (2.15)
Alejandro Perez (2.15)

Alejandro Perez/Ramone Sanchez

Lucia Perez/Marquez (2.15, 8.12)
Claudia Perez (8.11, 8.12)

John Rowland

Gabrielle Solis/Marquez (1.1, 1.2, 1.3, 1.4, 1.5, 1.6, 1.7, 1.8, 1.9, 1.13, 1.15, 1.18, 1.19, 1.20, 1.21, 1.22, 2.1, 2.3, 2.11, 2.16, 2.24, 3.3, 3.4, 3.13, 3.17, 4.3, 4.5, 5.16, 5.18, 5.20, 6.3, 6.4, 6.20, 719, 8.23)
Danielle Van de Kamp (1.6, 1.7, 1.8, 1.9, 1.15)
Joan Novak (2.3)
Tammy Sinclair (3.3, 3.17, 4.5, 6.3)
Ana Solis (6.3, 6.4)

Eddie Orlofsky

Susan Mayer (6.20)
Irina Korsakov (6.19)
Sex Worker (6.20)
Danielle Van de Kamp (6.20)

Irina Korsakov

Alexi Korsakov (6.19)
Preston Scavo (6.17, 6.18, 6.19, 6.22)
Eddie Orlofsky (6.19)

Jackson Braddock

Susan Mayer (4.17, 5.1, 5.2, 5.4, 5.5, 5.6, 5.7, 5.8, 5.9, 5.10, 5.11, 5.12, 5.13, 5.21, 5.22, 5.23)
Darcy (5.6)

David Dash/Williams

Lila Dash (5.1, 5.10, 5.11, 5.12, 5.14, 5.16, 5.17 5.23, 5.24)
Edie Britt/Williams (5.1, 5.2, 5.3, 5.4, 5.5, 5.6, 5.8, 5.9, 5.10, 5.11, 5.12, 5.13, 5.14, 5.15, 5.17, 5.18, 5.19, 5.20, 5.23)

Ian Hainsworth

Jane Hainsworth (3.1, 3.2, 3.9, 3.13, 3.14, 3.15)
Susan Mayer (3.1, 3.2, 3.3, 3.4, 3.6, 3.7, 3.8, 3.9, 3.10, 3.11, 3.13, 3.14, 3.15, 3.16, 3.17, 3.18, 3.19, 3.20)
Lynn (3.14)

Bob Hunter

Lee McDermott (4.4, 4.5, 4.6, 4.10, 4.14, 4.16, 4.17, 5.1, 5.3, 5.5, 5.8, 5.10, 5.11, 5.14, 5.17, 5.20, 6.2, 6.5, 6.10, 6.13, 6.16, 6.17, 6.18, 6.19, 7.2, 7.7, 7.9, 7.10, 7.12, 7.13, 7.16, 7.19, 7.21, 7.22, 7.23, 8.3, 8.7, 8.18, 8.20)

Lee McDermott

Bob Hunter (4.4, 4.5, 4.6, 4.10, 4.14, 4.16, 4.17, 5.1, 5.3, 5.5, 5.8, 5.10, 5.11, 5.14, 5.17, 5.20, 6.2, 6.5, 6.10, 6.13, 6.16, 6.17, 6.18, 6.19, 7.2, 7.7, 7.9, 7.10, 7.12, 7.13, 7.16, 7.19, 7.21, 7.22, 7.23, 8.3, 8.7, 8.18, 8.20)
Susan (5.11)
Tom Scavo (6.12)

Victor Lang

Samantha Lang (3.17)
Gaby (3.16, 3.17, 3.18, 3.19, 3.20, 3.21, 3.22, 3.23, 4.1, 4.3, 4.4, 4.5, 4.6, 4.7, 4.8, 4.9, 4.10)

Walter

Andrew (4.10)

Jane Hainsworth

Ian Hainsworth (3.1, 3.2, 3.9, 3.13, 3.14, 3.15)
Ted (3.13)

Juanita Solis

Diego Solis (1.5)

Julie Mayer

Zachary Young (1.6, 1.9, 1.10, 1.13, 1.15, 1.20, 2.4, 2.11)
Austin McCann (3.2, 3.3, 3.5, 3.7, 3.8, 3.10, 3.11, 3.12, 3.14, 3.16)
Derek (4.8)
Barrett (4.8)
Lloyd (5.8)
Danny/Tyler Bolen (6.1, 6.2, 6.9)
Nick Bolen (6.1, 6.2, 6.4, 6.5, 6.7, 6.8, 6.9)
Porter Scavo (8.14)

Austin McCann

Julie Mayer (3.2, 3.3, 3.5, 3.7, 3.8, 3.10, 3.11, 3.12, 3.14, 3.16)
Sarah (3.5)
Danielle (3.11, 3.12, 3.16, 4.15, 8.4, 8.9)

Zachary Young/Dana Taylor

Julie Mayer (1.6, 1.9, 1.10, 1.13, 1.15, 1.20, 2.4, 2.11)
Gaby (3.11, 3.12, 3.13, 3.14, 3.15)

Maisy Gibbons

Man #1 (1.10)
Man #2 (1.10)
Man #3 (1.10)
Rex Van De Kamp (1.10, 1.16)

Rodney Scavo

Lois (1.13)
Alison Scavo (1.13, 7.5)

Andrew Van De Kamp

Justin (1.15, 2.10, 2.11, 2.19, 2.21)
Peter McMillan (2.21)
Howard Keck (3.4)
The Beer Delivery Guy (3.18)
Walter (4.10)
Alex Cominis (5.10, 5.11, 5.12, 5.15, 6.16, 7.17, 8.18)
Tad (6.16)
Mary Beth (8.18)
Geoffrey with a G (8.18)
Bryan with a Y (8.18)

Morty Flickman

Sophie Bremmer (1.18, 1.21, 2.6, 2.8, 2.9, 7.12)
Dolores Flickman (1.21)

Danielle Van De Kamp/Katz

John Rowland (1.6, 1.7, 1.8, 1.9, 1.15)
Matthew Applewhite (2.7, 2.8, 2.13, 2.17, 2.20, 2.21, 2.22, 2.23, 2.24)
Robert Falati (3.4, 3.5, 4.1)
Austin McCann (3.11, 3.12, 3.16, 8.4, 8.9)
Leo Katz (5.1, 5.2, 5.3)

George Williams

Bree Van de Kamp (1.11, 1.12, 1.13, 1.20, 1.21, 1.22, 2.3, 2.4, 2.5, 2.6, 2.8, 2.9, 2.10, 2.24)
Leila Mitzman (2.8)
Unnamed woman 1 (2.6)
Unnamed woman 2 (2.6)
Unnamed woman 3 (2.6)

Matthew Applewhite

Danielle Van De Kamp (2.7, 2.8, 2.13, 2.17, 2.20, 2.21, 2.22, 2.23, 2.24)
Melanie Foster (2.14, 2.23)

Libby Collins

Frank Helm (2.17, 2.18)
Dale Helm (2.20)

Orson Hodge

Becky (2.19)
Susan (2.19)
Bree Van de Kamp/Hodge (2.23, 2.24, 3.1, 3.2, 3.3, 3.4, 3.5, 3.6, 3.7, 3.8, 3.9, 3.10, 3.11, 3.12, 3.13, 3.14, 3.15, 3.16, 3.23, 4.1, 4.2, 4.3, 4.4, 4.5, 4.6, 4.7, 4.8, 4.9, 4.10, 4.11, 4.12, 4.13, 4.14, 4.15, 4.16, 4.17, 5.1, 5.2, 5.3, 5.4, 5.5, 5.6, 5.7, 5.8, 5.9, 5.10, 5.11, 5.12, 5.15, 5.16, 5.17, 5.18, 5.19, 5.20, 5.21, 5.22, 5.23, 5.24, 6.1, 6.2, 6.3, 6.4, 6.5, 6.6, 6.7, 6.8, 6.9, 6.10, 6.11, 6.12, 6.13, 6.14, 6.15, 6.18, 6.19, 6.21, 6.22, 6.23, 7.1, 7.2, 7.6, 7.11, 7.19, 7.21, 8.2, 8.9, 8.13, 8.14, 8.15, 8.16, 8.19)
Alma Hodge (3.1, 3.2, 3.6, 3.7, 3.9, 3.10, 3.11, 3.12, 3.13, 3.14, 4.1)
Monique Polier (3.2, 3.6, 3.9, 3.10, 3.11, 3.12, 3.14, 3.15, 4.11)
Judy (7.1)

Andre Zeller

Ex-wife (8.6)
Amy (8.7, 8.8)

Barbara Orlofsky

Hank (6.20)
Ron (6.20)

Tim

Chloe (4.11)
Katherine Mayfair (4.11)

Dylan Mayfair

Bradley (4.17, 5.12)

Stella Wingfield/Lindquist/Kaminsky

Glen Wingfield (3.23, 4.8, 5.12)
Stan (4.7)
Affair (4.8)
Frank Kaminsky (7.13, 7.14)

Frank Kaminsky

Stella Wingfield/Kaminsky (7.13, 7.14)
First Wife (7.14)
Phyllis (7.14)

Glen Wingfield

Stella Wingfield (3.23, 4.8)
Dave (4.8)

Harvey Bigsby

Carolyn Bigsby (3.1, 3.6, 3.7)
Monique Polier (3.6, 3.7)
First Wife (3.7)

Karen McCluskey/Simonds/Bender

Gilbert McCluskey (3.5, 3.16, 3.18, 3.19, 3.20)
Roy Bender (6.1, 6.2, 6.5, 6.10, 6.12, 6.14, 6.15, 6.16, 6.18, 6.23, 7.7, 7.8, 7.9, 7.10, 7.15, 7.16, 7.17, 7.18, 7.19, 7.23, 8.14, 8.15, 8.16, 8.22, 8.23)
Tom Scavo (6.12)
College Boyfriend (7.17)

Juanita Solis

Ryan (8.13)

Roy Bender

Karen McCluskey (6.1, 6.2, 6.5, 6.10, 6.12, 6.14, 6.15, 6.16, 6.18, 6.23, 7.7, 7.8, 7.9, 7.10, 7.15, 7.16, 7.17, 7.18, 7.19, 7.23, 8.14, 8.15, 8.16, 8.22, 8.23)
Susan Delfino (6.16)
Blue hair (6.16)
Miriam (8.14, 8.15)

Bradley Scott

Maria Scott (5.11, 5.15, 5.26)
Shayla (5.15, 5.16)

Robyn Gallagher

Robyn and Bobby Butterfield (6.15)
Katherine Mayfair (6.15, 6.16, 6.17, 6.18, 8.23)

Porter Scavo

Anne Shilling (5.6, 5.7, 5.9, 5.10)
SarahJ/Lynette(5.2)
Tiffany (7.15)

Adam Mayfair

Katherine Mayfair (4.1, 4.2, 4.3, 4.5, 4.6, 4.7, 4.9, 4.10, 4.11, 4.16, 4.17)
Sylvia Greene (4.8, 4.9, 4.10)

Nick Bolen

Angie Bolen (6.1, 6.2, 6.3, 6.5, 6.6, 6.7, 6.8, 6.9, 6.10, 6.11, 6.14, 6.16, 6.17, 6.18, 6.19, 6.21, 6.22, 6.23)
Julie Mayer (6.1, 6.4, 6.5, 6.7, 6.8, 6.9)

Angie Bolen/de Luca

Nick Bolen (6.1, 6.2, 6.3, 6.5, 6.6, 6.7, 6.8, 6.9, 6.10, 6.11, 6.14, 6.16, 6.17, 6.18, 6.19, 6.21, 6.22, 6.23)
Patrick (6.11, 6.14, 6.17, 6.19, 6.21, 6.22)

Danny/Tyler Bolen

Julie Mayer (6.1, 6.2, 6.5, 6.9, 6.10, 6.12)
Ana Solis (6.2, 6.3, 6.9, 6.12, 6.13, 6.14, 6.15, 6.16, 6.17, 6.23)

Ana Solis

Danny/Tyler Bolen (6.2, 6.3, 6.9, 6.12, 6.13, 6.14, 6.15, 6.16, 6.17, 6.23)
John Rowland (6.3, 6.4)

Other

Norma and Leonard Harper (2.7)
Alisa and Dennis Stevens (1.17)
Ralph and Bonita (2.12)
Eleanor and Henry Mason (2.19)
Fran and Ed Ferrara (2.10, 2.20, 2.21)
Vera and Howard Keck (3.4)
Tania and Durkin (3.8)
Graham and Dahlia Hainsworth (3.17)
Mayor Johnson and Sydney (3.21)
Al Kaminsky and Wife (4.10)
Walter and Todd (4.10)
Reverend Green and Carolyn (4.16)
Carolyn and her Korean Grocer (4.16)
Clay and Girlfriend (5.6)
Rose Kemper and Husband (5.20)
Helen and Ed (5.19)
Fran and Mark Shulman (5.22)
Heidi and Don Bremer (6.5)
Denise "Moose" Lapera and Mark Malone (6.7)
Emily and Nick (6.8)
Terrence and Crystal (6.8)
Daphne Bicks and Jeff Bicks (6.10)
Trisha Reed and Husband (6.10)
Walter and Shirely Lackey (6.14)
Louise McMullen and Bobby Butterfield (6.15)
Mary and Richard Watson (7.8, 7.9)
Carmen and Hector Sanchez (7.4, 7.8, 7.9, 7.11)
Tracey and Adam Miller (7.9)
Richard and Tracey (7.9)
Emma Graham and Husband (7.5)
Doug and Tina (7.5, 8.14)
Lisa and Andy (7.22)
Lee and Tom Mankiewicz (7.22)

Lydia and Rashi/Herbert Brickmeyer (8.3)
Jackson and Jenny (8.3)
Franklin and Cindy (8.8)
Steve and Jennifer (8.23)
Nick and Adele Delfino (8.16)
Henry and Mrs. Mason (8.17)
Henry Mason and Secretary (8.17)
Doris and Bill Hammond (8.20)

First Date

Mike and Susan go to Bree's dinner party together (1.3)
Mike asks Susan out again to a Billy Wilder retrospective (1.4)
Mike ends up taking Edie out on a date (1.4)
Susan and Officer Thompson (1.5)
Mike and Susan plan their first overnight date (1.8)
Edie Britt and Karl Mayer (1.11)
Bree and George Williams (1.11)
Bill and Susan (1.17)
Susan and Jim Halverson (2.12)
Bree and Detective Barton (2.12)
Ian and Susan (3.2)
Gaby and Zach (3.13)
Gaby and Luke (3.14)
Victor and Gaby (3.16)
Mike and Susan's first date gets cancelled when Kendra turns up (1.7)
Mike and Date (5.6)
Katherine and Peter Hickey (5.6)
Frank and Lynette (8.12)
Tom and Lynette (8.17)

Affairs

Karl Mayer and Brandy (1.1, 5.19)
Gabrielle Solis and John Rowland (1.1)
Rex Van de Kamp and Maisy Gibbons (1.10)
Susan and Karl (2.19)
Andrew and Peter McMillan (2.21)
Carlos and Xiao-Mei (2.23)
Edie and Folk Singing Duo (3.6)
Harvey Bigsby and Monique Polier (3.6)
Orson Hodge and Monique Polier (3.2)
Austin and Danielle (3.11)
Ted and Jane (3.13)
Sarah and the Mailman (3.20)
Gaby apologizes to Carlos for having an affair (2.3)
Carlos hints at Lynette that he wants to have an affair (2.11)
Addison's wife thinks Susan is having an affair with her husband (2.10)
Bree tells Lynette about Gaby's affair with John (2.11)
Tom finds out that Lynette fell in love with Rick (3.22)
Gaby tells Father Crowley that Carlos and Sister Mary are having sex (2.13)
Tom suspects that Lynette and Rick are having an affair (3.20)
Tom asks Rick if he is having an affair with Lynette (3.21)
Rick and Lynette reveal their feelings for each other (3.21)
Mike kisses susan after she has a fight with Ian (3.18)
Nora reveals that she is trying to win Tom back (3.5)
Brandy apologizes to Susan for having an affair with Karl (1.3)
Tom tells Lynette about Kayla (2.23)
Gaby and Carlos (4.1)
Edie figures out that Carlos and Gaby are having an affair (4.4)
Carlos tells John he forgives him for having an affair with Gaby (4.5)

John tries to start up his affair with Gaby again (4.5)
Edie tells Victor about Gaby and Carlos' affair (4.6)
Stella Wingfield and unnamed partner (4.8)
Adam Mayfair and Sylvia Green (4.9)
Tim and Katherine Davis/Mayfair (4.11)
Ellie's mother (4.16)
Lynette thinks Tom is having an affair with Anne Shilling (5.6, 5.7)
Porter and Anne Shilling (5.6, 5.7, 5.9, 5.10)
Edie reveals that her father had an affair (5.12)
Bradley and Shayla (5.15, 5.16)
Edie and Ed (5.19)
Bree and Karl (5.24)
Julie Mayer and Nick Bolen (6.1)
Orson finds out about Bree's affair (6.8)
Orson finds out that Bree is having an affair (6.10)
Gaby and Bree (7.19)
Renee thinks Ben is having an affair with Bree (8.9)
Claudia accuses Susan of having an affair with Ramone (8.12)

Marriage Proposals

Carlos proposed on his and Gaby's third date, shown in a flashback (1.1)
John proposes to Gabrielle (1.13)
Sophie Bremmer and Morty (1.21)
George asks Bree to marry him (2.7)
Karl asks Edie (2.18)
Mike buys Susan a ring (2.23)
Orson asks Bree (3.1)
Ian asks Susan (3.15)
Zach asks Gaby (3.15)
Victor asks Gaby (3.19)
Susan asks Mike (3.21)
Edie thinks Karl is proposing (2.15)
Edie asks Carlos (4.2)
Edie tells the girls that she and Carlos have discussed marriage (4.1)
Gaby asks Carlos (4.11)
Bradley asks Dylan (4.17)
Lloyd proposes to Julie (5.8)
Jackson asks Susan to marry him (5.21)
Mike proposes to Katherine (5.22)
Karl proposes to Bree (6.6, 6.10)
Preston proposed to Irina (6.17)
Roy proposes to Karen (6.16)
Eddie proposes to Susan (6.20)
Chuck was going to propose to Bree (8.3)
Keith Watson is going to propose to Bree (7.9)
Keith proposes to Bree (7.10)
Ben proposes to Renee (8.12)

Engagements

Mike and Susan discuss marriage (2.6)
Tom and Anabel Foster (1.20)
Sophie Bremmer and a man who liked to gamble (1.21)
Sophie Bremmer and a man who liked to drink x2 (1.21)
Sophie Bremmer and a man who liked other men (1.21)
Sophie Bremmer and Morty (1.21)
George and Bree (2.7)
Susan and Gary Grantham (2.14)
Susan and Karl (2.14)
Karl and Edie (2.18)
Orson and Bree (3.1)
Ian and Susan (3.15)
Victor and Gaby (3.19)
Susan and Mike (3.21)
Edie and Carlos (4.2)
Bradley and Dylan (4.17)
Alex and Andrew (5.10)
Susan and Jackson (5.21)
Mike and Katherine (5.22)
Roy and Karen (6.16)
Preston and Irina (6.17)
Frank and Stella (7.13)
Lydia and Rashi (8.3)
Renee and Ben (8.12, 8.18)
Andrew and Mary Beth (8.18)

Engagement Parties

George and Bree (2.7)
Edie and Karl (2.18)
Orson and Bree (3.1)
Gaby and Victor (3.20)
Jackson and Susan (5.22)

Weddings/Commitment Ceremonies

Carlos and Gaby wedding night (1.9)
Sophie and Morty (2.8)
Susan and Gary Grantham (2.14)
Susan and Karl (2.15)
Bree and Orson (3.2)
Gaby and Victor (3.23, 4.2)
Susan and Mike (3.23)
Edie plans a surprise wedding with Karl (2.18)
Bree writes her wedding thank you cards in a flashback (1.8)
Katherine and Wayne (4.11)
Gaby and Carlos (4.11)
Bob and Lee (4.17)
Arminian Wedding (5.1)
Edie and Dave (5.12)
Susan and Jackson (5.22)
Mike and Katherine (5.24)
Susan and Mike (5.24, 6.1, 6.20)
Unnamed Couple (5.24)
Bree and Tripp (8.23)

Break Ups

Karl and Susan Mayer (1.1)
Rex and Bree Van de Kamp (1.3)
Gabrielle Solis and John Rowland (1.7, 1.8)
Mike and Susan (1.8)
John Rowland and Danielle Van de Kamp (1.9)
Bree and Rex Van de Kamp (1.10)
Karl Mayer and Brandy (1.11)
Gabrielle Solis and John Rowland (1.13)
Susan tells Zach he is forbidden from seeing Julie (1.13)
Bree Van de Kamp and George Williams (1.13)
John Rowland and Danielle Van de Kamp (1.15)
Susan and Mike (1.15)
Sophie Bremmer and Morty 1.18
Julie and Zach (1.20)
Tom and Anabel Foster (1.20)
Gaby leaves Carlos (1.22)
Mike and Susan (2.6)
Karl and Edie (2.7)
Bree Van de Kamp and George Williams (2.8)
Susan and Dr. Ron (2.17)
Susan and Karl (2.19)
Edie and Karl (2.20)
Bree Van de Kamp and Peter McMillan (2.21)
Lynette leaves Tom (2.22)
Matthew Applewhite and Melanie Foster (2.23)
Gaby and Carlos (2.24)
Nora and Turk (3.2)
Gaby and John (3.3)
Susan and Mike (3.4)
Ian and Susan (3.4)
Danielle and Robert Falati (3.5)
Carlos and Gaby (3.7)
Bree and Orson (3.9)

Mike and Edie (3.10)
Gaby and Bree (3.11)
Orson and Alma - flashback (3.12)
Austin and Julie (3.12)
Gaby and Luke (3.14)
Gaby and Zach (3.15)
Austin and Julie (3.16)
Ian and Susan (3.19)
Ian and Mike (3.20)
Ian and Susan (3.20)
Rick and Lynette (3.21)
Edie and Carlos (3.23)
Gabrielle tries to separate Danielle and John (1.7)
Gaby and Victor (3.23)
Gaby and Carlos (4.5)
Edie and Carlos (4.6)
Gaby and Victor (4.6)
Adam and Katherine (4.10)
Bree and Orson (4.13, 6.10)
Orson moves out (4.14)
Susan and Mike (4.17)
SarahJ/Lynette and Porter (5.2)
Susan and Jackson (5.5)
Anne and Porter (5.9)
Anne Schilling and husband (5.9)
Susan and Jackson (5.12)
Edie and Dave (5.11)
Edie and Umberto (5.13)
Karl and Susan (5.13, 6.11)
Mike and Susan (5.13)
Susan and Jackson (5.13)
Karl and Marisa (5.18)
Susan and Jackson (5.23)
Bree and Orson (5.23, 6.23)
Mike and Katherine (6.1)
Julie and Nick (6.5, 6.7)

Bree and Karl (6.6)
Carlos and Gaby (6.11, 7.19)
Bob and Lee (6.19)
Preston and Irina (6.19)
Renee and Doug (7.1, 7.5)
Paul and Beth (7.6, 7.15)
Keith and Stephanie (7.3)
Mary and Richard (7.7, 7.8)
Keith and Bree (7.10, 7.15)
Judy and Orson (7.11)
Alex and Andrew (7.17)
Lynette and Tom (7.23, 8.1)
Chuck and Bree (8.3)
Danielle and Leo (8.4)
Renee and Ben (8.12, 8.14)
Katherine and Robin (8.23)
Greg and Lynette (8.21)
Tom and Jane (8.21)
Andrew and Mary Beth (8.18)

Divorced

Rex and Bree announce their separation (1.7)
Bree tells Rex she is going to divorce him (1.10)
Karl and Susan (2.24)
Carlos and Gaby (3.7)
Mike and Susan (5.5)
Orson asks Bree for a divorce (5.5)
Marie asks Bradley for a divorce (5.11)
Edie and Umberto (5.13)
Bree starts divorce proceedings against Orson (5.21)
John Rowland and Tammy Sinclair (6.3)
Tom and Lynette both sign divorce papers (8.19)
Lynette and Tom divorced (8.22)

Back Together

Mike and Susan get back together and have sex for the first time (1.8)
Karl asks Susan to get back together (1.11)
Rex and Bree Van de Kamp (1.14)
Sophie Bremmer and Morty (1.21)
Mike and Susan (1.21)
Bree Van de Kamp and George Williams (2.2)
Karl and Edie (2.7)
Karl and Susan (2.19)
Mike and Susan (2.23)
Gaby and John (3.3)
Carlos and Gaby (3.7)
Ian and Susan (3.6)
Orson and Bree (3.10, 6.12)
Austin and Julie (3.16)
Ian and Susan (3.20)
Mike and Susan (3.21)
Karl kisses Susan and asks her to take him back (2.18)
Karl tells Susan he loves her (2.19)
Gaby tries to rekindle her relationship with Carlos to benefit from his new job (3.6)
Mike kisses susan after she has a fight with Ian (3.18)
Lynette tells the kids that her and Tom have separated (2.23)
Sister Mary encourages Carlos to get an annulment (2.13)
Gaby and Victor (3.23)
Gaby and Victor (4.6)
Katherine asks Adam to get back together, but he declines (4.11)
Bree and Orson (4.17)
Susan and Jackson (5.6)
Edie and Dave (5.12)
Mike and Susan (5.24)

Bree and Karl (6.6)
Karl and Susan (6.11)
Renee and Doug (7.5)
Paul and Beth (7.6)
Bob and Lee (7.7)
Keith and Bree (7.11)
Karen and Roy (8.15)
Tom and Lynette (8.22)
Bree and Tripp (8.23)

Moved in Together

Rex moves back home with Bree (1.7)
Mike and Susan (1.22)
Carlos moves back home (3.4)
Edie and Carlos (3.22)
Mike and Susan (3.22)
Susan and Mike don't move in together (2.1)
Karl buys Susan a house (2.23)
Carlos moves out (3.9)
Stella and Glen (4.8)
Jackson asks Susan to move in together (5.5)
Alex Cominis and Andrew Van de Kamp (5.9)
Jackson wants susan to move in with her (5.11)
Mike and Katherine (5.15, 5.16)
Jackson and Susan (5.22)
Katherine and Robyn (6.15)
Keith and Bree (7.10, 7.11)
Tom and Jane (8.16)

Pregnancies

Lynette (1.1, 5.13, 5.24
Gabrielle (1.18)
Xiao-Mei (2.22)
Lynette (2.23)
Alma (3.10, 3.12)
Danielle Van De Kamp (3.16)
Bree (3.23)
Edie pregnancy scare (3.22)
Edie and Carlos decide to have a baby (3.22)
Orson reveals that Alma had a miscarriage (3.10)
Gaby loses her baby (2.7)
Susan (4.1)
Tammy Rowland (4.5)
Gaby (5.5)
Anne Shilling (5.7)
Maria (5.15)
Anna (5.17)
Lynette loses one of her babies (6.11)
Lisa Ellison (7.9)
Julie Mayer (8.13)

Says "I Love You'

Mike and Susan (1.11)
David tells Gaby he is in love with her (2.6)
Bree tells George the polygraph showed she was in love with him (2.3)
George tells Bree he loves her (2.6)
Doctor Ron tells Susan (2.16)
Caleb Applewhite tells Melanie Foster he loves her (2.14, 2.23)
Justine tells Bree he loves Andrew (2.19)
Ian tells Susan he loves her (3.4)
Edie tells Mike when she first laid eyes on him, she fell in love with him (3.6)
Victor tells Gaby he is in love with her (3.18)
Austin and Julie say they are in love (3.12)
Gaby realises John is in love with her (1.2)
Susan tells Dr. Ron she loves Mike (2.16)
Carlos tells Edie he's not in love with her (3.22)
Jackson tells Susan he's falling in love with her (5.5)
Mike says he's falling in love with Katherine (5.12)
Karen tells Roy she loves him (6.2)
Bree tells Karl she is is falling in love with him (6.6)
Karl tells Bree he loves her (6.6)
Danielle tells Matthew she loves him (2.20)

Couples in Counselling

Bree and Rex start marriage counselling (1.2)
Tom organises a secret couple's therapy session (3.22)

Sex

Lynette says Tom and her got kicked out of Disneyland for lude behaviour (1.3)
Gaby and Carlos broke a waterbed in Cancun when she wore spiked heels (1.3)
Bree reveals that Rex cries when he ejaculates (1.3)
Bree and Rex start to have sex, but stop when she becomes distracted (1.6)
Bree realises that Rex's problems are due to his dissatisfaction with their sex life (1.6)
John and Gabrielle get together for break up sex and get discovered (1.7)
Justin tries to blackmail Gabrielle into having sex with him (1.14)
Rex and Bree try domination together (1.14)
George and Bree sleep together (2.6)
Karl and Susan sleep together (2.7)
Carlos and Edie sleep together (3.17)
Edie and Mike have sex for the first time (3.6)
Julie and Austin have sex for the first time (3.11)
Alma rapes Orson (3.13)
Bree and Orson have sex for the first time (3.1)
Susan said she has had 11 lovers (3.3)
Susan and Ian have sex for the first time (3.3)
Mike sees Susan naked (1.3)
Zach fools Gaby into thinking they slept together (3.14)
Gaby tells Susan that if she was a lesbian, she would 'totally do' her (3.22)
Bree goes to second base with her boyfriend in a flashback (1.8)
First mention of Gaby being molested by Alejandro (1.9)
Tim and Katherine sleep together (4.11)
Juanita sees her parents having sex (5.4)

Katherine and Peter Hickey (5.6)
Jackson and Susan start a casual relationship (5.5)
Katherine hasnt had sex in two years (5.6)
Bree and Karl won't be having sex for a month (6.6)
Katherine said Mike and her had sex 5 times in one day (6.8)
Gaby had sex with Mick Jagger (7.14)
Susan having sex dreams about Paul (7.19)
Tom and Lynette sleep together (8.1)
Gaby and Carlos haven't had sex for 39.5 days (8.2)
Mike and Susan like having sex in public (8.2)
Susan walks in on Tom and Lynette having sex (7.9)
Renee tells Lynette about sleeping with Tom (7.11)
Frank and Lynette have sex (8.13)
Lynette offers Mike sex (8.15)

Meeting the Parents

Susan meets Ian's parents (3.10)
Susan meets Mike's mother (4.15)
Julie brings Lloyd home to meet Susan (5.8)
Andrew brings home Alex (5.10)

Other Significant Events

Susan finds out about Karl and Edie (2.2)
Car Wash was Mike and Susan's song (3.5)
Susan promises Ian she won't see Mike anymore (3.10)
Ian and Mike bet Susan in a card game (3.16)
Gaby and Carlos declare that they are leaving (4.9)
Bob and Lee in counselling (6.13)
Tom and Lynette in counselling (6.13)
Katherine and Robyn are outed (6.18)

Secrets and Lies

Season One

Karl Mayer and Brandy's affair (1.1)
Gabrielle Solis and John Rowland's affair (1.1)
Mrs Huber keeping Mary Alice's blender (1.1)
Karl's affair with Brandy (1.1)
Why Mary Alice shot herself (1.1)
What's under the Young's pool (1.1)
John and Gaby's Affair (1.1)
How Edie's house got set on fire (1.1)
How the Solis' front lawn really got mowed (1.1)
Why Mike really moved to Wisteria Lane (1.1)
Mary Alice's real dress size (1.1)
What Mary Alice did (1.1)
Why Gaby had taken another shower (1.2)
Where John was and what he was wearing (1.2)
Where the measuring cup is (1.2)
Why John gave Gaby the rose (1.2)
What's in the chest Paul put into the lake (1.2)
Where Rex is really sleeping (1.3)
What Tom really got up to on his business trip (1.3)
Where Rex really is (1.4)
Where Andrew really was last night (1.4)
Mary Alice's real name (1.4)
Where the sock under Carlos' bed really came from (1.4)
When the cable guy got to the Solis house (1.4)
What the Mary Alice note was really about (1.4)
Who sent Mary Alice the note (1.4)
What really happened to Juanita Solis' husband (1.5)
Who broke into Mrs Fromme's house (1.5)
Where the screwdriver really went (1.5)
Where the Van de Kamp car really went (1.8)

Why Lynette is really looking so tired (1.7)
Who Dana is (1.6)
Where Victor really collapsed (1.7)
What Susan was really doing at the SaddleRanch (1.7)
What Juanita was doing on Wisteria Lane (1.7)
Who hit Juanita Solis (1.7)
What's wrong with Lynette's eyes (1.7)
Who killed Martha Huber (1.8)
Why Mike has a gun and money in the cabinet (1.8)
What Mike's relationship is to Kendra (1.7)
What Zach did, that made Mary Alice want to kill herself (1.5)
Why Rex really feels sexually disconnected from Bree (1.6)
Why Mike has all that cash and a gun (1.8)
Why Susan really wanted to be alone in Mike's house (1.8)
Who is really having an affair with John (1.9)
What Gaby's step father did to her (1.9)
Andrew's drug use (1.9)
Maisy Gibbon's day job (1.10)
Who is in Susan's house (1.10)
Rex Van de Kamp and Maisy Gibbons's affair (1.10)
Where Zach has been hiding (1.10)
Why Gaby needs to store her household items (1.10)
Who brought Rex to the hospital (1.10)
What happened to Martha Huber (1.11)
What Rex did to cause Bree to be so angry (1.11)
Where Carlos's passport is (1.11)
How long Karl had actually been acting disrespectfully in his marriage to Susan (1.11)
Why Noah needs Mike to hurry up (1.12)
What Porter is sick with (1.12)
Why Susan is really going with Edie (1.12)
Who wrote the note to Mary Alice (1.7)
Who Gaby is having an affair with (1.6)
Where Zach really is (1.6)
Carlos tampering with Gaby's birth control pills (1.12)
Where Bree went (1.13)

Tom's fathers infidelity (1.13)
Why Bob is so nice to Gabrielle (1.13)
Why Susan really offered to chaperone the dance (1.13)
What Zach has told Julie (1.13)
What George is going to do with Rex's prescription (1.13)
What Susan really heard in Julie's phone call with Zach (1.13)
What Tom did, that Lynette can't find out about (1.13)
How Gabrielle really feels about John (1.13)
Whose condom was in the hamper (1.15)
What happened to Dana (1.6)
How Mike really got shot (1.14)
How Martha Huber's bracelet got into Mike's garage (1.14)
What Rex is into sexually (1.14)
Where Mrs. McCluskey's clock went (1.14)
Why Justin really wants to mow the Solis's lawn (1.15)
Who really killed Martha Huber (1.15)
Why Tom didn't get the VP promotion (1.16)
Why John was really broke up with Danielle (1.16)
Why Justin was blackmailing Gaby (1.16)
Who Patient Zero is (1.17)
Who was in the swimming pool (1.16)
Mike's police record (1.16)
Why Gaby has to keep using other people's bathrooms (1.16)
Why Gaby and Carlos aren't prioritising the plumbing (1.16)
Who is in Maisy's little black book (1.16)
What Edie was really doing in Paul's house (1.16)
Why Tammy Brennan really uninvited the Scavo twins (1.16)
What is in Mike's letter (1.17)
How Juanita Solis actually died (1.17)
How Alisa's husband talks about her behind her back (1.17)
Susan's date with Bill (1.17)
Carlos's tampering with Gaby's birth control (1.18)
How old Susan's mother really is (1.19)

Where Gaby got the money for the shoes (1.19) '
What Gaby's real name is (1.19)
Why Mrs. McCluskey hasn't been answering the door (1.19)
Who else has been invited to dinner (1.19)
Why Bree wants Andrew to change who he is (1.19)
Andrew's birth complications (1.19)
What Sullivan got paid to give Mike the homicide case file (1.19)
What Andrew's true intentions for Bree are (1.19)
Where Carlos is going (1.20)
How long Annabel has been working with Tom (1.20)
George secretly still in love with Bree (1.20)
How Martha Huber found out about what the Young's did (1.20)
Where Paul's VHS tape really is (1.20)
Why Gaby is having trouble with the smell of meat (1.20)
How Gaby really got pregnant (1.20)
Who set Susan's house on fire (1.20)
Bree's decision to see George without telling Rex (1.20)
The truth behind Angela/Mary Alice's name change (1.21)
What Bree needs to talk to Edie about (1.21)
Why Zach feels so unwell (1.21)
Why Felicia hasn't seen Zach for a while (1.21)
What's going on between Bree and George (1.21)
How scared Felicia actually was when she was talking to Paul (1.21)
Why Gaby really slapped Justin (1.22)
Why Lynette really keeps showing up at Tom's office (1.22)
George's true feelings (1.22)
How George know about Rex's sexual preferences are (1.22)
Why Mike will really be missing dinner (1.22)
Why the Applewhite's don't want Edie doing an inspection (1.23)
Why Susan won't let Edie in (1.23)
Where Mike really is (1.23)

Where Tom has been when Lynette thought he was at work (1.23)
Who Dana really is (1.23)
Who Zach's real mother is (1.23)
Who Zach's father is (1.23)
Who killed Deirder (1.23)
Who Rex thought poisoned him (1.23)

Season Two

Rex's mother sneaking the prep school tie on (2.1)
Karl and Edie have been dating for six months (2.2)
What Karl said to Susan, the day he asked Edie out (2.2)
Who is in the Applewhite's basement (2.1)
What the noise is in the Applewhite's basement (2.2)
What Karl said to Edie in the jacuzzi (2.2)
What Betty really wants the prescription for (2.2)
Where the mouse came from (2.2)
Phyllis calling the insurance company (2.2)
What was on Betty's top (2.3)
John's relationship with Joan (2.3)
Why Matthew was really playing loud music (2.3)
Bree is in love with George (2.3)
Why Lynette keeps trying to leave the meeting (2.3)
Susan hiding that she found Zach (2.4)
What Susan did when she found Zach (2.4)
Where Mrs. Mulberry went (2.4)
What Lonny really did at his firm (2.5)
How Rex felt in his final moments (2.5)
Why Mike lied to the police (2.6)
When Lynette actually bought the suit (2.6)
Lynette didn't return the suit (2.6)
How Bree got so drunk (2.6)
What Bree really wanted to say when George proposed (2.7)
Why Edie and Karl really broke up (2.7)
The depth of Norma and Leonards's movie hobby (2.7)
George organised an engagement party (2.7)
How Bree gets her flowers to look so good (2.7)
What Matthew was really looking for in the Van de Kamp backyard (2.7)
What Susan said to make Karl go back to Edie (2.7)
What George did to Dr. Goldfine (2.7)

Gaby's pregnancy (2.7)
Who is in Gaby's House (2.7)
Where Caleb is (2.7)
Who Susan's father is (2.8)
What Gabrielle is really feeling, after the miscarriage (2.8)
The truth about George and Leila (2.8)
Where Susan's father is (2.8)
Who hurt Bree's therapist (2.9)
What Susan's relationship to Addison is (2.9)
How hot Sister Mary is (2.9)
Who Nina is sleeping with (2.9)
Why Stu was really fired (2.9)
Bree's involvement in George's death (2.9)
What sister Mary's motivation is (2.9)
The extent of George's obsession with Bree (2.10)
Who the 'mystery vagrant' is (2.10)
Why Bree released Andrew from 'kid jail' (2.10)
What kind of friend Justin is (2.10)
Where the church got the money to send Sister Mary (2.10)
What Andrew's plan is for his mother (2.10)
How George really died (2.10)
What Betty is really doing at the hospital (2.10)
Who really killed Martha Huber (2.11)
What Andrew's relationship with Justin really is (2.11)
The depth of Bree's drinking problem (2.11, 2.12)
What Monroe is really doing on Wisteria Lane (2.11)
Gaby's history with John (2.11)
Who hired Monroe (2.11)
How Carlos felt about his kiss with Lynette (2.11)
How Monroe's body got in the trunk of the car (2.11)
Zach figures out who his biological father is (2.12)
Mike didn't kill Todd/Paul (2.12)
Why Tom is really avoiding the chicken pox (2.12)
Susan's symptoms (2.12)
Why Felicia has taken the job as Noah's nurse (2.12)
Why Edie really tied Karl up (2.13)

Tom is Lynette's husband (2.13)
Gaby's 'confession' about Carlos and Sister Mary's relationship (2.13)
Who is in Betty's upstairs window (2.13)
Why Sister Mary is being transferred (2.13)
What Bree was really going to tell the girls about Betty (2.13)
How Maxine really pulled off the cooking (2.14)
Why Gaby really wants Xiao-Mei to stay (2.14)
Where Caleb has been living all these months (2.14)
Were Susan's wedding ring really went (2.15)
Who Carlos is upstairs with (2.15)
Why Lynette really doesn't need Mrs McCluskey (2.15)
Why Bree passed out on the front lawn (2.15)
How Bree really lost the Scavo boys (2.15)
Susan's residual feelings for Karl (2.15)
Carlos's conversation with Gaby's mother (2.15)
Bree was hiding her drinking (2.16)
How Susan feels about Dr. Ron (2.16)
Who really bruised Andrew (2.16)
Who Mike is (2.17)
Why Donovan really gave up breastfeeding (2.17)
Karl and Susan's lingering feelings (2.18)
Why Bree really went over to Lynette's (2.18)
What Edie's engagement party really is (2.18)
Who Libby's baby belongs to (2.18)
Karl and Susan's marriage (2.18)
What Karl really told Edie (2.19)
Mike's feelings for Susan (2.19)
Susan and Karl's affair (2.19)
Why all these accidents are happening to Paul (2.19)
Ed has been thinking about hookers (2.20)
Why Claude really had the drugs on him (2.20)
Who Karl was really seeing on the side (2.20)
Matthew manipulating Caleb (2.20)
Who was really messaging Fran (2.20)

Danielle's real response to Caleb's visit (2.20)
What Betty is going to do to Caleb (2.21)
Andrew and Peter McMillan's affair (2.21)
Susan's relationship with Karl (2.21)
Why Tom really hit Ed (2.21)
What Matthew really told Caleb about Danielle (2.21)
Why Tom has been going to Atlantic City (2.21, 2.22)
Where Caleb really is (2.21)
Why Peter really left dinner (2.21)
How Xiao-Mei thought she would become impregnated (2.21)
Why Mike really paid off the private investigator (2.21)
Peter and Andrew sleep together (2.21)
How Susan's house went on fire (2.21)
Who burned Susan's house down (2.22)
Who ate some of the cake frosting (2.22)
What really happened to Andrew (2.22)
Where Matthew has been (2.22)
Carlos's sandwich (2.22)
How Gaby got her room back (2.22)
Where Lynette really is (2.22)
What happened to Felicia Tilman (2.22)
Where Bree really is (2.23)
Who really killed Melanie Foster (2.23)
Who Mike's ring is really for (2.23)
How Noah died (2.23)
Carlos and Xiao-Mei's affair (2.23)
Why Karl really bought Susan a house (2.23)
Who ran over Mike (2.23)

Season Three

What happened to Alma (3.1)
Where Xiao-Mei went (3.1)
Where the birthday party is (3.1)
Who the body belongs to (3.1)
What Susan and Ian are really doing at the restaurant (3.2)
How Nora got at the table with the 'stiffs' (3.2)
How Orson knows the body at the morgue (3.2)
Orson Hodge and Monique Polier's affair (3.2)
How Andrew ended up on the streets (3.3)
How many women Ian has had sex with (3.3)
Susan's 'magic number' (3.3)
Why Nora was so upset about Lynette's comment (3.3)
John's engagement (3.3)
Where the diamond watch really came from (3.3)
What Andrew did for money (3.3)
Where Andrew really was (3.4)
How Parker really got that shot (3.4)
How Bunny Conners got Chlamydia (3.4)
What Andrew did with Vera's husband (3.4)
Danielle and her relationship with her history teacher (3.4)
Gaby's weekend with John Rowland (3.4)
Why Howard really wasn't home (3.4)
Mike's true feelings for Susan (3.4)
Lynette's feelings about Tom's dream (3.4)
Why Robert broke up with Danille (3.5)
What Julie did to Austin's assignment (3.5)
Why Carolyn really apologised (3.6)
Edie's affair with a Folk Singing Duo (3.6)
Harvey Bigsby and Monique Polier's affair (3.6)
The truth about Carlos' new job (3.6)
Where Orson's mother really is (3.8)
Why Gaby really didn't go back to modeling (38)
What's in Art's basement (3.8)

What Tom is really going to Mike's for (3.9)
What Orson did (3.9)
Who Gloria is calling (3.10)
The truth about Art (3.10)
Why Austin isn't pressuring Julie for sex (3.11)
Who sent Gaby's flowers (3.11)
Why Gaby really wants to stop at the florist (3.11)
Austin and Danielle having sex (3.11)
Susan seeing mike in jail (3.11)
Julie's trip to the doctor for birth control (3.12)
Julie having sex (3.12)
How Lynette got the liquor license (3.12)
Who has been sending things to Gaby (3.12)
Why Sherri won the pageant (3.13)
Ted and Jane's affair (3.13)
Paul paying off the prisoner (3.13)
Why Lynette really wasn't at work (3.13)
What really happened the night Monique died (3.14)
Who really tampered with Bree's ladder (3.14)
Why Gaby's date really left (3.14)
What really happened between Gaby and Zac (3.15)
Who really made Bree's soup (3.15)
How Orson's mother really got beside Alma's body (3.15)
How Victor got Gaby to come back (3.16)
How Ian knew about the ring inscription (3.16)
What Ian's father is doing with women's clothing (3.17)
Why Ian's father did not ask Susan to sign the pre-nup (3.17)
Where Gaby got the dress for the party (3.17)
Why Edie sent Travers to bed early (3.17)
Kayla's crush (3.18)
Why Rick wants to 'slum it at a pizza joint' (3.18)
Why Ian really wants to relocate (3.18)
What happened at Mike's (3.18)
Who Carlos is seeing (3.19)
What is in Karen's freezer (3.19)
Why Lynette really couldn't come home from work (3.20)

Sarah and the Mailman (3.20)
Where Susan and Lynette really are (3.20)
Why Lynette doesn't want to fire Rick (3.20)
Why Tom wants to come back to work (3.20)
What Rick and Lynette were doing when Scavo's was robbed (3.21)
Why Edie bought the puppy (3.21)
Tom and Rick's lunch (3.21)
Why Rick left (3.21)
What Victor organised for the meter reader (3.21)
Why Mrs Simms canceled Carlos' lease (3.22)
Gaby stole Susan's whole wedding (3.22)
Lynette's feelings for Rick (3.23)
Edie's birth control regime (3.23)
Why Victor really married Gaby (3.23)
Bree's pregnancy (3.23)
Susan's plans for the wedding (3.23)
Where Danielle really is (3.23)

Season Four

What Ede's true plan was (4.1)
Gaby and Carlos's affair (4.1)
Susan's wedding (4.1)
Lynette's tumour (4.1)
Brees make believe pregnancy (4.1)
Why Gaby won't sell her house (4.1)
Carlos' bank account (4.1)
Why Dylan doesn't remember living on Wisteria Lane (4.1)
What happened in that room (4.1)
Who was responsible for the crime spree (4.2)
Why Katherine really had to move (4.2)
Which Lemon Meringue pie was really being served (4.2)
Susan's decision about Julie going to the party (4.2)
Why Gabrielle didn't want to go to Lyentte's chemo treatment (4.2)
Why Gabrielle 'can't' come to Charades night (4.3)
Why Bree lied to Susan about who her doctor was (4.3)
Why Carlos had to get engaged to Edie (4.3)
What Lily and Katherine covered up (4.4)
The baby shower (4.4)
Where Raphael really was (4.4)
Why Gaby couldn't start up her affair with John again (4.5)
Why Carlos really left Edie (4.6)
Mike's father: dead or alive? (4.6)
Who had really given birth to Benjamin (4.7)
Who Gaby was really talking to on the phone (4.7)
Mike's drug dependency (4.7)
Benjamin's circumcision (4.7)
What happened to Victor (4.7)
Where Stella is (4.8)
Stella Wingfield's affair with unnamed partner (4.8)
How Mike knows Barrett (4.8)
Mike's drug problem (4.8)
Why Stella and Glen broke up (4.8)

Why Andrew is mad (4.8)
What Victor remembers (4.8)
Orson already knew about Mike's drug problem (4.9)
Adam Mayfair and Sylvia Green's affair (4.9)
What was written on the piece of paper (4.10)
The reality of Carlos' condition (4.10)
Why Gaby really went to Al's (4.10)
Where Carlos got Edie's bracelet (4.11)
Tim and Katherine's relationship (4.11)
What's in Gaby's beef stew (4.11)
Why Bree wants the Scavo's to come back to church (4.11)
Why Gaby really wanted Carlos to come on her errands trip (4.12)
What Bree knew about what Katherine ate (4.12)
Why Katherine is presenting the award (4.12)
Who started the fire at Rick's (4.13)
Why Dylan really got pulled up (4.13)
What Elie does in her room with men (4.14)
Whose idea it was to set fire to Rick's (4.14)
Why Susan made Mike dress up for Lamaze class (4.14)
Where Orson spent the night (4.14)
Who Dylan really belongs to (4.15)
Who Benjamin really belongs to (4.15)
Who Dylan really is (4.15)
How Susan really got a wet leg (4.15)
Susan changes MJ's name (4.16)
How Kayla really got that burn (4.16)
Where Adam went (4.16)
What's in Ellie's teddy bear (4.17)

Season Five

Porter and Preston's poker nights (5.1)
Jackson and Susan's relationship (5.1)
Why Dave's doctor checks in with him once a month (5.1)
How Jackson knew about 'the ear thing' (5.2)
Who is really talking to Porter on Silverfizz (5.2)
Why Gaby is taking Carlos to the party through the kitchen (5.2)
Bree crying in the kitchen (5.2)
Where Toby went (5.2)
Who is bullying MJ (5.3)
Tom's Playboy magazines (5.3)
How Tom's bass got left on the garage floor (5.3)
What Bree fed Benjamin (5.3)
Where Dave went to college (5.3)
Where Orson has been going during the day (5.4)
How MJ learned to ride his bike (5.4)
Why MJ fell off the bike (5.4)
What Gaby and Carlos were really doing when Juanita walked in (5.4)
What Bree's success is costing her (5.4)
Why Gaby can't talk to Bob and Lee (5.5)
How Gaby could be pregnant (5.5)
Bree's alcoholism while Orson was in prison (5.5)
Carlos' desire for another child (5.5)
How Carlos' really got so much in tips (5.6)
Porter and Anne Shilling's affair (5.6)
What Tom was doing with Ann Shilling (5.6)
Who the condom at the band's rehearsal space belongs to (5.6)
How Orson knows Peter (5.6)
Why Tom is really leaving the house (5.6)
Ann Shilling's pregnancy (5.7)
Katherine and Mike's relationship (5.7)
Everyone having sex in Bree's test kitchen (5.7)

Why Jackson doesn't want to have sex (5.7)
What happened to Dr. Hellyer (5.8)
Why Dave really saved Mike from the fire (5.8)
The truth about Ann's pregnancy (5.8)
What Lynette knows about where Ann went (5.8)
Who Mike is seeing (5.9)
Where the Scavo's emergency fund went (5.10)
What happened to Carlos' baseball (5.10)
Why Lynette is really going into Edie's bedroom (5.10)
Who Dave is talking to (5.11)
Where Porter is (5.11)
What happened between Lee and Susan (5.11)
Why Alex walked out of the meal at Bree's (5.11)
The witness who placed Porter in the store room (5.14)
How much Mike paid for Katherine's pearls (5.14)
How much Bree is paying Andrew (5.15)
Bradley and Shayla's affair (5.15)
Why Tom has called the family meeting (5.15)
What Orson is really doing, making Bree come up with a porn name (5/25)
Why Bradley gave Carlos his bonus (5.15)
What really happened to Susan's painting (5.16)
Orson's stealing (5.16)
How the priest knows Dave (5.16)
Dave's real name (5.16)
Why Susan really took the painting back (5.16)
Why Gaby wants Lynette to take the job (5.17)
Why Dave wants Katherine and Mike to go camping (5.17)
Dave's real intentions (5.18)
Why Edie had her accident (5.18)
Edie visiting Orson (5.19)
How Orson got injured (5.20)
The truth about Lynette's two showers (5.20)
Who was really driving when Mike and Susan crashed (5.20)
What Dave is planning for MJ (5.20)
Why MJ was asking about marriage (5.21)

Why Jackson proposed to Susan (5.21)
Bree's break in (5.22)
The real reason Jackson and Susan are getting married (5.22)
Why Tom wants to go to college (5.23)
Why Tom almost missed his test (5.23)
Why Aunt Connie wanted everyone to come over (5.23)
The truth about Ana (5.23)
Who reported Jackson to immigration (5.23)
Who really texted Susan (5.23)
What's on the tape Dave gave Mike (5.23)
How the Solis house got so clean so quickly (5.24)
Why Lynette is feeling so unwell (5.24)
Bree and Karl's affair (5.24)
Who Mike is marrying (5.24)

Season Six

Susan putting Katherine in the closet (6.1)
Julie Mayer and Nick Bolen's affair (6.1)
How Angie got burned (6.1)
Who hurt Julie (6.1)
Julie thinking she was pregnant (6.2)
Lynette's pregnancy (6.2)
Where Ana really was (6.2)
Nick and Angie's real names (6.3)
The mailman hits his wife (6.4)
The nice woman across the street embezzles (6.4)
The attractive couple that jog by every morning use cocaine (6.4)
Julie dropped out of college to be a waitress (6.4)
Who "D" is (6.4)
Where Bree really was when Orson called (6.5)
Where Susan's 'lost' brooch went (6.6)
Why Tom bought the keg (6.6)
Where Bree got the brooch (6.6)
Why Bree really wanted Angie's recipes (6.7)
Why Tom and Lynette are trying to put Terrence and Crystal off Florida (6.8)
Why Susan is insisting on having sex so much (6.8)
What Gaby told Carlos (6.8)
Who killed Emily (6.8)
Who stabbed Katherine (6.9)
Karl's business (6.12)
Which of the animal groups is the advanced group (6.13)
Tom's feeling journal (6.13)
Angie and Danny's sexual relationship (6.13)
Why Susan wants to crack Mike's back (6.15)
Katherines feelings for Robin (6.15)
Gaby broke up Danny and Ana (6.15)
Why Gaby really didn't want to come back home (6.16)

Where Danny really is (6.16)
Why Katherine didn't want to go shopping (6.17)
Why Irina is really with Preston (6.17)
Who Sam's father is (6.17)
Who Danny's father is (6.17)
Why Gabrielle really left modeling (6.17)
Why Irina really gave the ring back (6.17)
Why Preston's bed had really been unmade (6.18)
Katherine's relationship with Robin (6.18)
Why MJ didn't sell any candy on the last day (6.18)
What Patrick's story is really about (6.19)
What Irina's phone call was about (6.19)
Why Mike won't let Susan pay for the truck (6.19)
Why all the residents on Wisteria Lane needed plumbing (6.19)
Who damaged Bree's food (6.19)
Who Eddie likes (6.20)
Eddie's Scrapbook (6.20)
Who hit Nick (6.21)
Mike's loan from Carlos (6.21)
How Sam knows Lillian (6.21)
Susan and Gaby's prank (6.21)
Where Eddie's mother really is (6.22)
Where the bomb really is (6.23)
What family is raising a baby that isn't theirs (6.23)
Who rented Susan's house (6.23)

Season Seven

Carlos and Gaby's baby was switched at birth (7.1)
Gaby and Carlos's secrets from each other (7.1)
What Felicia has planned (7.1)
Why Paul has moved back to Wisteria Lane (7.2)
Why Gaby pretends to have sexsomnia (7.2)
Why Bree really fired Keith (7.2)
Why Beth wrote about sex in her letters (7.2)
What happened between Tom and Renee (7.2)
Why Juanita has type A blood (7.2)
How Bree's sprinkler system really got broken (7.3)
What Lynette did to Tom's marijuana (7.3)
Gaby contacting Bob to find the family (7.3)
Bree's real feelings about the Black Eyed Peas (7.4)
How Danielle came to be at Bree's (7.4)
Why Penny was taking the baby monitor into her room (7.4)
Gaby giving grace the necklace (7.4)
Where Mike and Susan's money went (7.5)
Gabrielle's nose job (7.5)
Why Bree really wanted Keith to get the work done in one day (7.5)
Keith's female roommate (7.5)
Why Gaby likes Grace so much (7.6)
Why Bree fainted (7.7)
Bree's real hair colour (7.7)
What Paul is doing (7.7)
Why Susan is upset about the job (7.7)
How Bree and Keith's mother know each other (7.7)
Why Carlos canceled his trip with Bob (7.7)
Who Beth's mother is (7.7)
Hector and Carmen's immigration status (7.8)
What Keith was planning for Thanksgiving (7.8)
Who rang immigration (7.9)
Why Lynette doesn't tell the women about Tom's penis (7.9)

Who Renee is in love with (7.9)
Who shot Paul (7.10)
Gaby's letter (7.10)
Why bad things are happening to Tom (7.11)
How many children Gabrielle really has (7.11)
Why Judy and Orson really broke up (7.11)
Gaby's doll (7.12)
Why Susan's mother can't be a donor (7.12)
Who the flower delivery man was (7.12)
How Bree really knew about Amber (7.12)
Why Stella is really marrying Frank (7.13)
The real reason Dick is so mean (7.13)
Keith's real feelings about Charlie (7.13)
What Paul was really planning at the cabin (7.13)
What Mike knows about Zach's location (7.14)
Who really shot Paul (7.14)
Why Monroe is really donating his kidney (7.14)
Why Susan really needed to bump the line at the supermarket (7.15)
What Gaby told the nun (7.15)
Where Juanita's shoes really went (7.15)
Where Lynette's baby is (7.16)
Where Susan is getting her kidney from (7.16)
Andrew's drinking problem (7.17)
How the car really got into Carlos' driveway (7.17)
Why Renee was really throwing the party (7.17)
Where Beth's ashes really ended up (7.18)
What Susan dreamed about (7.19)
Gaby and Bree's secret relationship (7.19)
Karen saw Felicia the night she framed Paul (7.19)
Who made the pineapple upside down cake (7.19)
Where Gaby is really going (7.19)
What Felicia is doing to Paul's food (7.20)
Why Gaby's kids are really being so helpful (7.20)
Why Chuck really came to Bree's house (7.20)
What Carlos really told the girls (7.20)

Why Felicia won't taste the food (7.20)
How the principal knew what Susan was wearing in Va Va Broom (7.21)
Who was outside the tent (7.21)
Where Felicia really went (7.22)
Why Chuck doesn't want to sleep with Bree yet (7.22)
What kind of man Paul really is (7.22)
Who was following Gaby at the supermarket (7.22)
Where Tom really went (7.23)
How the dinner got burned (7.23)
What's really on the candlestick (7.23)

Season Eight

What Bree and Gaby are really doing in the car (8.1)
Who really took the car (8.1)
Why Susan is really upset about Cupcake (8.1)
What Susan isn't telling Mike (8.1)
Who sent the note (8.1)
Why Renee hates charity work (8.2)
What Bree was really going to tell Chuck (8.2)
Who Jackson is (8.3)
What really changed Rashi's mind (8.3)
Susan and Carlos working together (8.3)
What Chuck has planned (8.3)
Why Tom is really whitening his teeth (8.4)
What Danielle is really selling (8.4)
Why Lynette really bought the device for Penny (8.4)
Who Tom is really seeing (8.4)
What Bree and Gaby were really talking about (8.6)
How the eggs really got on Ben's house (8.6)
Who really made Penny's costume (8.6)
How Renee got her allergic reaction (8.6)
Why Penny doesn't want to see Tom (8.7)
Why Juanita and Celia acted so well during dinner (8.7)
Why Juanita graffitied the garage (8.7)
Why Carlos is really home (8.8)
Why Susan doesn't want her painting at the gallery (8.8)
Why Gaby is at Jimmy's group counselling (8.9)
Where Carlos went (8.10)
Who ran over Chuck (8.10)
Why Susan is really looking at the house (8.11)
Why Ben is really making time for Renee (8.11)
Who really owns the house with the pool (8.11)
What Ramone was doing to his step daughter (8.11)
Why Ben really proposes (8.12)
Julie's pregnancy (8.13)

Julie's plans for her baby (8.13)
Where Juanita's valentine really came from (8.13)
Who is watching Bree (8.13)
Where Carlos really is (8.13)
How Orson really knew where Bree was (8.13)
Who the father of Julie's baby is (8.14)
Who exploded Ben's construction site (8.14)
Why Karen broke up with Roy (8.14)
Roy's real feelings about going home to Karen (8.14)
What the girls really said to Orson (8.14)
Orson following Bree (8.14)
Why Tom wants Jane to become a bigger part of his life (8.16)
What's in Karen's pie (8.16)
Why Bree represses her feelings (8.16)
Why the police really questioned Bree (8.16)
Why Andrew is really marrying Mary Beth (8.18)
Lynette and Penny's plan (8.18)
Why Lynette's lights are really out (8.18)
Why Tom doesn't want to have sex with Jane (8.18)
What's in the locked box in the closet (8.19)
Who Jenny Hernandez is (8.19)
How Bree's address got onto the paper from Ramone's motel room (8.19)
MJ's real feelings about the go kart (8.20)
Why Ben has been subpoenaed (8.20)
Bree's feelings about Tripp (8.20)
What Gaby did to Carlos' office (8.20)
Why Renee testified against Bree (8.22)
Who Lynette is in love with (8.22)
Susan moving (8.22)
What's in the box (8.23)

Documents in *Desperate Housewives*

The pilot for Desperate Housewives ends with the housewives discovering an important note, written on a piece of lavender paper. It is realised by the women that the note may have played a significant factor in Mary Alice's suicide, and the viewer spends much of season 1 trying to figure out what role the note played in her death.

This note was the first of many important notes, letters, and other documents that serve as important plot elements across the eight seasons. This section represents a small selection of these documents. Some of these are replica's, while others are images of actual props used on the show. In one way or another, every piece in this chapter was an important document in moving the narrative along.

Letter from Martha Huber to Mary Alice Young, and from Orson to Bree
(1.1, 3.7, 5.13, 7.1, 8.1, 8.2)

I KNOW WHAT YOU DID

IT MAKES ME SICK

IM GOING TO TELL

Note from Orson to Bree (8.10)

You're

Welcome

Orson envelope at end of ep (8.15)

Fairview Police
Homicide Division
2511 East 6th Street
Fairview, Es. 00057

Mrs Huber Missing Flyer (1.11)

OFFICIAL PUBLICATION OF THE FAIRVIEW POLICE DEPARTMENT

MISSING

NAME:	Huber, Martha
MISSING:	December 12, 2004
AGE:	48
SEX:	Female
DESCENT:	German, Caucasian
HEIGHT:	5'13"
WEIGHT:	120
HAIR:	Brown
EYES:	brown
MISSING FROM:	Fairview
REPORT #:	01-141536

Circumstances:

Missing person (MP) was last seen on December 12, 2004 from Wisteria Lane, in Fairview. The MP disappeared under unusual circumstances. The MP has short brown wavy hair, pale complexion, and a mole on her left arm. MP's mental and physical condition is described as good.
Clothing description is unknown.

If you have any information about this person or their whereabouts, please

contact detectives at:

Fairview Police Department
151 A. Wain St, Fairview, Eagle State, 25102

Note from Felicia to Paul (1.21)

Paul –

Zach is with me

Felicia

Note from Paul to Zach (1.22)

Zach,

I didn't leave you.
Meet me at the baseball field -
Thursday at midnight.
                          Dad

Rex note to Bree (1.23, 2.5)

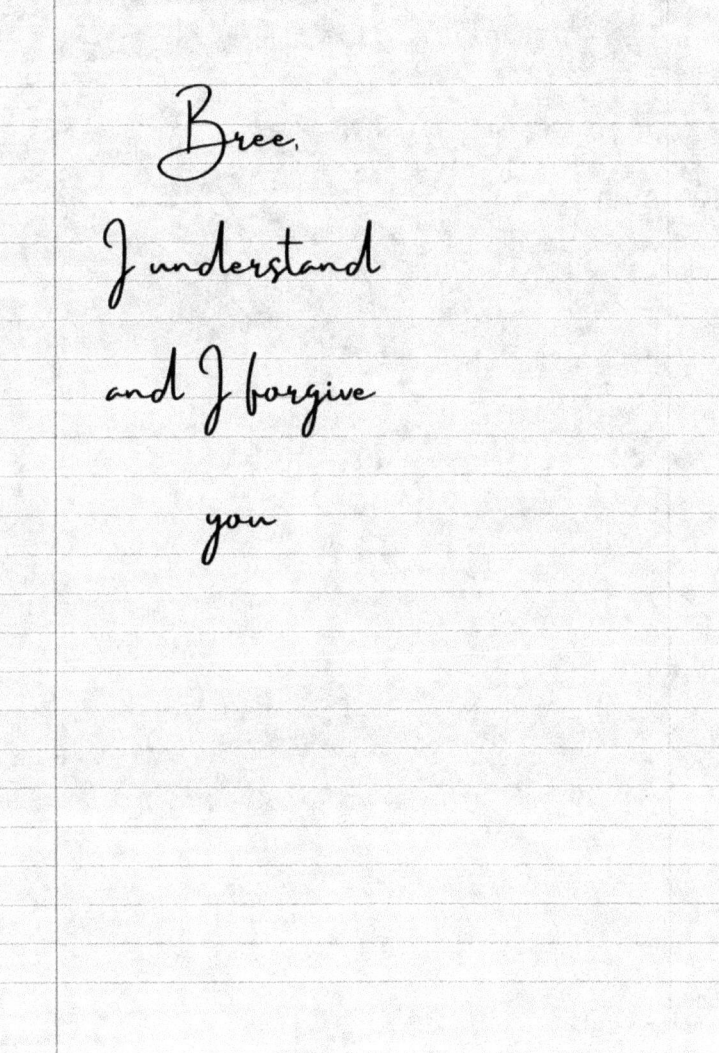

Letter from Betty Applewhite to the Police (2.5)

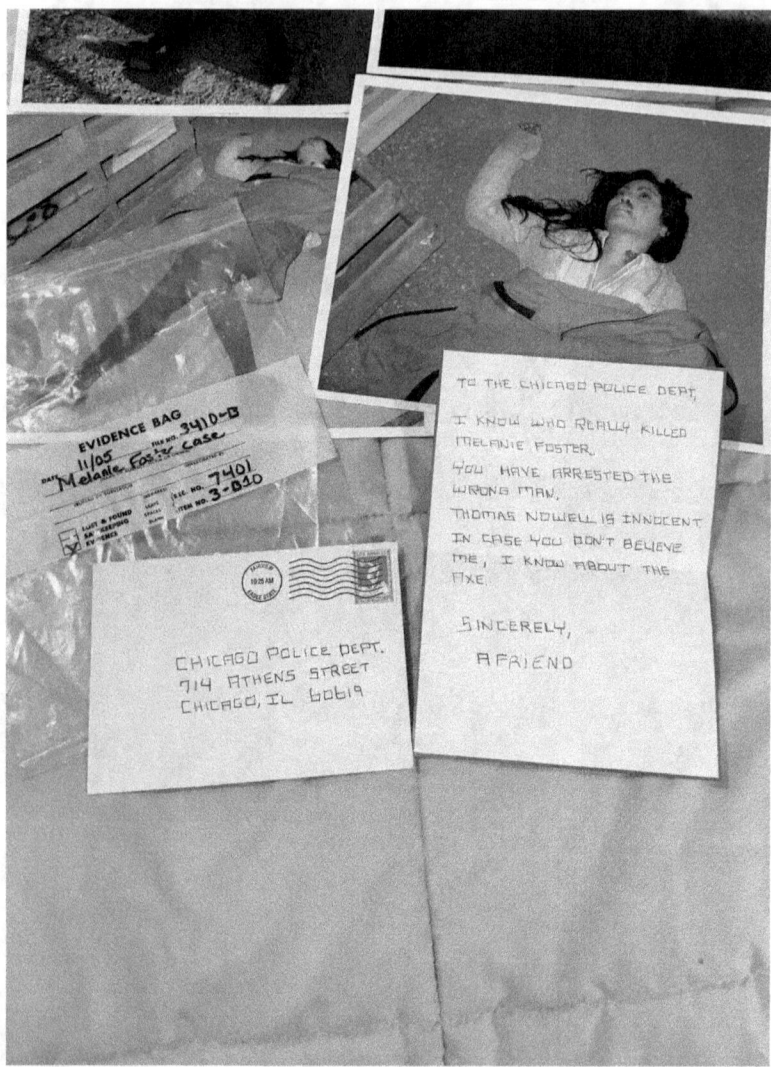

George note to Bree (2.9)

Bree,

I can't live with you thinking im a bad person. I've taken some pills. If you could do me one last kindness, please come up and say goodbye. I'm in room #617

George

Gabrielle's DNA results (2.1)

DNA TESTING

GENETIC TEST REPORT

NAME:	Gabrielle Solis	**Case / Test No:**	555555 - 000000
ADDRESS: :	4349 Wisteria Lane	**Customer Number:**	06 - D6
	Fairview, ES USA		

		Registration #	Match
Mother:	SOLIS, GABRIELLE	12456	99.9%
Child:	SOLIS, BABY	12457	99.9%
Alleged Father:	SOLIS, CARLOS :	12458	99.9%

Conclusion:

Orchid Cellmark's DNA analysis has determined that CARLOS SOLIS is the biological father of BABY SOLIS to a liklihood of 99.99%.

Susan's note to Karl in the Restaurant (2.15)

> Be careful!
> She thinks you're
> about to propose.

Note from Lynette to Bree (2.15)

> Do you still think you don't have a problem?

Danielle's note to Bree (2.22)

Mother,

Matthew and I are running away together and we're never coming back. If you want me to be happy you won't try to find us.

Living in that house with you...was like being in a prison. You drove me to do this, so I hope you blame yourself.

Have a nice life,

Danielle.

Susan's invitation to Mike (2.24)

BRING SOME CHAMPAGNE AND YOUR HEART ♥ AND MEET ME AT 8:30 AT LOVER'S POINT ON TORCH LAKE XOXO SUSAN

Alma's faked suicide note (3.15)

> Orson,
>
> I thought I could make you love me again, even after the terrible thing I did. I was wrong. If I can't live with you I don't want to live at all.
>
> alma

Orson Suicide Rough Draft 12:50

Dearest Bree,

I will always love you, but the will to fight on has left me, so I've chosen to exit life on my own terms.

Scavo's Menu
(3.6, 3.11, 3.12, 3.13, 3.14, 3.15, 3.16, 3.17, 3.18, 3.20, 3.21, 3.22, 4.1, 4.8, 4.12, 4.13, 4.16, 5.1, 5.3, 5.5, 5.6, 5.10, 5.14, 5.15, 5.16, 7.20)

Movies Referenced in the Show

A Streetcar Named Desire
(7.11) Orson calls Keith Stanley Kowalski

Finding Nemo
(1.3) Tom and Lynette have 45 minutes until the kids actually find Nemo

The Shawshank Redemption
(6.6) Gabrielle says, "What is this? Shawshank Elementary?"

Bambi
(1.6) Lynette references this when confronting Maisie at the school play

Lassie
(1.8) Susan tells Bongo that Lassie would have gotten her help

Norma and Leonard 7/1/05
(2.7) The kids are watching this in the Scavo boys bedroom

Rods: The Hunter You'll Want to Catch
(2.19) This video was in Andrew's porn box

Pollyanna
(7.13) Dick calls Susan Pollyanna

Pinocchio
(7.5) Lee tells Gaby not to lie or her nose will grow

Bloody Stranger 2
(7.21) Juanita watches this with Gaby

Rain Man
(8.19) Lynette says she is like Rain Man

His Girl Friday
(5.12) Lynette's mother is watching this

Caddyshack
(8.21) Trip says he is more of a *Caddyshack* kind of guy

Wizard of Oz
(8.6) Susan says "I do believe in spooks"
(7.4) Lynette said Renee freaks out everytime this is on T.V.

Fatal Attraction
(3.5) Edie said think of this, with a much older woman

The Three Stooges
(7.7) Bree asks Renee if she's ever laughed at at Three Stooges movie
(8.23) Gaby asks Carlos to name his price, and includes a Three Stooges marathon as a suggestion
(6.8) Mike asks if he can turn this on while he and Susan have sex

Cinderella
(3.9) Susan is compared to her, when she loses her shoe at the start of the episode

Seabiscuit
(3.15) Carlos calls Zach Seabiscuit

The Americanization of Emily
(4.3) Lynette got this in 15 seconds

Two Mules for Sister Sara
(4.3) Bree guesses this at Charades

Hang 'Em High
(4.3) Lynette gets this in Charades

Sports Blooper DVD
(4.1) This is on Lynette's nightstand

Stepford Wives
(1.1) Andrew says Bree is the one always running for the mayor of Stepford

Scooby Doo
(4.13) Carlos says his dog Roxy can "solve crimes with Shaggy and the gang"

Shrek
(5.1) The store clerk says she bets there is a Mrs. Shrek dress that would fit Juanita

Surf's Up
(5.7) The Solis family are watching this for family movie night

Woody Woodpecker
(7.5) Bree can't keep up with Keith's "Woody Woodpecker sex drive"

Rear Deployment
(5.10) Alex was in this porn movie

Snow White and the Seven Dwarfs
(5.20) Andrew asks if Orson will "whistle while he works"

Love Lessons
(7.5) Paul gives this to Beth

Peter Pan

(5.22) Tom calls Bill Peter Pan
(7.9) Tom and Lynette have sex "in front of Peter Pan"

Batman
(5.22) tom calls bruce the joker

Dave Home Video
(5.23) Mike plays this at the airport

Bruce Lee Movies
(5.22) Susan asks if Tom is going to watch these without subtitles

Air Bud
(6.16) Gaby asks if the movie Bob and Lee rented has a dog who plays basketball

Downtown Girl
(6.16) Bob and Lee rent this

Happy Feet
(6.16) Gaby asks if the movie Bob and Lee rented has a talking penguin

Brian's Song
(4.2) Lynette said sitting with Tom during her chemo treatments was like the last 20 minutes of this movie
(6.17) Mike cried during this movie

The Notebook
(6.17) Mike cried during this movie

Willy Wonka
(6.18) Gaby calls Susan Willy Wonka

Mommie Dearest

(4.17) Bob says Lee is acting like Faye Dunaway from the boardroom scene in this movie
(6.16) When Juanita calls Gaby says she has to "do the Mommie Dearest thing"

A Tramp and the Lady
(6.20) This is guessed at charades

My Fair Lady
(6.20) This is guessed at charades

Spiderman
(2.11) Lynette calls Paul Young 'our friendly neighbourhood murderer'

Du Barry Was a Lady
(6.20) This is guessed at charades

Psycho
(7.5) When Keith opens the shower, Bree says "Please tell me you're here to stab me"

Mary Poppins
(2.4) Tom said that Parker really locked into the whole Mary Poppins thing

Willard
(2.2) Lynette is watching this when she sleeps on the couch

Coming Home
(2.10) Title Reference

So Proudly We Hail!
(2.13) Edie is watching this when Karl changes the channel

Dreamgirls

(8.7) The Solis girls sing a number from this for Bob and Lee (8.7)

Dumbo
(8.2) Susan says the policeman's baby has Dumbo ears

Braveheart
(8.4) Gaby asks if the parents have seen this movie

300
(8.4) Gaby asks if the parents have seen this movie

Nanook of the North
(6.8) Gaby calls Lynette 'Nanook'

Citizen Kane
(8.10)The Scavo's fell asleep during this
Casablanca
(8.10) The Scavo's fell asleep during this
(8.12) Tripp brings this over to Bree's to watch

Marty
(8.10) The Scavo's fell asleep during this

Fatal Attraction
(7.14) Susan tells Monroe that there is close and then there is "Glenn Close"

Old Yeller
(8.10) Tom got this out for family movie night

Fictional movie about a parrot who coaches an inner city debate team
(8.11) Mike jokes that Susan watched this on the way back

Fictional movie about a dolphin who joins an inner city water polo team
(8.11) Susan watched this on the plane

The Godfather
(8.15) Renee says the loan shark has crawled out of a Godfather movie

John Wayne films
(7.5) Bree says she has a John Wayne walk

Cheech and Chong movies
(7.3) Carlos calls Tom Cheech

Hitchcock
(1.4) Mike asks Susan to a Hitchcock retrospective

Musicals and Theatre Referenced in the Show

Gypsy
(1.4) The cable guy has a poster of this on his wall
(5.17) Orson steals a mug with this on it

Aida
(2.7) Bree said her and George saw this and cried buckets

Pippin
(2.17) Susan said she was in this at school

Fiddler on the Roof
(4.3) Stella said Lynette's performance in this was so bad even alcohol couldn't block it out

Brigadoon
(4.5) Lee says Susan butchers the score to this

West Side Story
(4.14) Lee says he played Tony in this musical

Cyrano de Bergerac
(7.5) The girls were making jokes about this to Gaby

Madame Butterfly
(6.8) Karl and Bree see this opera

Cats
(7.7) Gaby bought Bob tickets to this

Annie
(7.7) Lee saw this six times

Gilbert and Sullivan
(6.14) Orson asks the two men if they are Gilbert and Sullivan fans

Judy Garland's concert at Carnegie Hall
(7.10) Lee wants to go back for a program that was signed at this concert

Wicked
(8.7) Tom and Jane are taking Penny to this

West Side Story
(8.7) Juanita's "favourite musical"

Dreamgirls
(8.7) The Solis girls sing a number from this for Bob and Lee (8.7)

Avenue Q
(6.8) Angie asks Orson if he has ever seen this

TV Shows Referenced in the Show

Wacky Races
(3.9) The Scavo kids are watching this when Lynette falls asleep

Punk'd
(4.5) Gaby thinks the art on Lee and Bob's front lawn is part of this show

Cagney and Lacey
(7.14) Frank calls two of the Scavo kids Cagney and Lacey

Mexican Soap Opera
(1.5) Juanita is watching this every day

Guiding Light
(4.14) Karen says Ida will wander into her house drunk when this is on

What's Cooking, Fairview?
(5.1) Fictional show that covers Bree's catering company

The Donna Reed Show
(5.8) Sandra calls Bree a "Donna Reed housewife"

Project Runway
(6.5) Lee puts his hand up for a Neighbourhood Watch patrol, but Bob reminds him that it is during this show

Unnamed Soap Opera
(6.16) This is playing on Katherine's television

Nightline

(7.3) Bree said tonight's episode looked interesting

Xena: Warrior Princess
(1.11) Gaby is offered a modeling job as a warrior princess at a sci-fi convention

Lost
(1.17) Andrew is watching this when Bree asks him to take out the trash

American Playhouse: Sunday in the Park with George
(1.21) Title reference

Twin Peaks: Episode 1.7
(3.1) The parrot's line mimics Waldo's line from this episode

I Love Lucy
(7.8) Gaby says that Carlos will go all "Ricky Ricardo" on her ass
(8.3) Mike says Susan called Carlos "Ricky Ricardo" for years

Looney Tunes
(7.11) Keith quotes Yosemite Sam
(8.4) Lynette quotes this when Tom has his teeth whitener in

Tom and Jerry
(7.15) MJ wants to get home to watch this

Gabrielle's Closet
(8.23) Gabrielle's television show

The Andy Griffith Show
(3.9) Lynette calls the detective Barney Fife

MTV's Beach House
(8.2) Lynette said Tom makes his visitation seem like this show

The Bachelor
(6.8) Susan tells Mike ton hurry up because this show is on

Music Referenced in the Show

Artists

Elvis Costello
(1.5) Mike's favourite band (guy with a band)
(2.24) Susan has this queued up
Joni Mitchel - Reference - Susan says if Mike had kept her CD...
Aerosmith - Tom wants to play bass in this band (3.3)
Elvis (7.17) Andrew tells AA that is his name
Blue Odyssey (5.6, 5.8, 5.23) The husbands band
Cold Splash (5.8) Another band at the Battle of the Bands
Wham (4.14) Gaby says Lee looks like the lost member from this band
Black Eyed Peas (7.4) Keith buys tickets for a BEP concert
The Supremes (6.4) Tom calls Lynette's breasts The Supremes
Cher (4.6) Bree helps Andrew dress like Cher for Halloween
(7.23) Lee says "Heavens to Cher"
Ricky Martin (8.3) Lee yells this out to test the masseur
Bob Geldof (8.4) Discussion of him can be heard on the television when Danielle is watching
Barry White - Lynette says she isn't putting Barry White on while she showers (5.20)

Songs

You Belong With Me (8.18) Penny tells Lynette about this song
Whistle While You Work (5.20) Andrew asks if Orson will "whistle while he works"
Desperate Housewives Theme - plays every episode
Mazzy Star- Fade Into You - This plays when Susan is telling her friends about Karl's affair (1.1)
Ave Maria (1.17) A singer performs this at Juanita's funeral
Isn't She Lovely (1.9) Plays during the fashion show
This Little Light of Mine (2.3) Julie sings this at Edie's, and at the concert
Rhinestone Cowboy (2.11) This is playing in Monroe's car
Peter Gunn (2.11) Monroe's ringtone
Gaby (3.13) Zach wrote this, and sings it for Gabrielle
Dust in the Wind (1.13) Susan and Paul dance to this at the school dance
Waltzes, Op. 69: No. 2 In B Minor (Waltz No. 10) This plays during dinner at Bree's (1.3)
Do It (Let Me See You Shake) - This plays while Edie washes her car (1.4)
Rough & Ready - This plays at the bar. (1.7)
All Night Long - This plays at the bar. (1.7)
Fireball - This plays at the bar. (1.7)
Wind Beneath My Wings (3.20) Lynette says that Susan has written a poem, which reworks the lyrics to this song
Let's Misbehave (3.13) Alma puts this on while she rapes Orson
Bennie and the Jets (6.4) Tom calls his private parts this
Old Macdonald Had a Farm (6.15) Katherine says someone at the hospital sang this everyday
Let's Get It On (1.1) This song is playing at Edie's when the fire starts
The 59th Street Bridge Song (Feelin' Groovy) (1.8) This plays while Lynette is having her vision

Boogie Shoes (2.5) Lynette dances to this at the bar
Boom Boom (2.5) Plays in the bar
Band of Gold (2.5) Plays in the bar
Good Lovin' (3.18) Plays while Gaby and Victor have sex in the limo
Break On Through (To the Other Side) (5.1) Orson sings this
I Wanna Be Your Boyfriend (5.1) Jackson sings this
Smoke On the Water (5.3) Tom plays this
Dead Man's Party (4.6) Plays at the Halloween party
Cello Suite No. 1 in G Major, BWV 1007: I. Prélude (4.4) Plays when Aunt Lily is dying
Forty & Above (4.2) Plays at the party Susan takes Julie from
Another Night (4.2) Plays at the party Susan takes Julie from
Set it Off (1.17)
I Know What Boys Like (5.19) Plays during Edie and Gaby's competition at tbe bar
Turandot: Nessun dorma (5.11) Lee is listening to this
In a Cave (5.8) The youth band is playing this
Mustang Sally (5.8) Blue Odyssey play this
The Nutcracker, Op. 71: XIIb. Character Dances: Coffee (Arabian Dance) (6.15) Bree tries to seduce Orson
(I Love You) For Sentimental Reasons (6.14) This plays at the anniversary party
Warbonnets & Wingsuits (6.14) Plays while Anna is coming down from Danny's room
Silent Night (6.10) The choir sings this
All I Wanna Do (6.20) This can be heard playing in the bar
Madame Butterfly (6.8) Plays when Bree comes home
The Ballad of Millicent Marmer (6.8) Plays while Danny is fixing the car
You Spin Me Round (6.1) Plays at the club when Gaby looks for Ana
My Funny Valentine (7.23) Renee sings this on the piano
Push It (7.22) Plays at the gay bar
Joy to the World (6.10) This is playing at the Christmas festival
Margaritaville (6.23) Tom sang this when he was drunk

Lucy in the Sky with Diamonds (7.3) Tom says he is Lucy in the sky high
Fo Sheezy (7.11) Orson asks which Lil Wayne song is Bree's favourite
Ask Dem Hoes (7.11) Orson asks which Lil Wayne song is Bree's favourite
Voodoo Child by Jimi Hendrix (5.4) Donald plays this for his band audition
Hotel California (5.6) Blue Odyssey is practicing this
Don't Give Up On Us (2.9) George sings this to Bree
Don't Cha? (2.17) This is playing at Libby's strip club
You Are So Beautiful (2.19) Karl has the band play this for Susan
Hava Nagila (2.19) The band plays this
Wonderful, Wonderful (8.23) This plays in Karen's last moments
Give a Little Bit (2.18) Plays when Bree is drunk
Stone Free (2.18) Plays when Bree goes to the bar
Il Trovatore / Act 2: Per me, ora fatale i tuo momenti affretta (2.15) Plays at the restaurant
Il Trovatore / Act 3: "Ah sì ben mio" (2.15) Plays at the restaurant
My Funny Valentine (2.15) Plays when Edie thinks Karl is going to propose
Bridal Chorus (3.2) This plays at Bree and Orson's wedding
Car Wash (3.5) Susan plays this for Mike in hospital
Julie, Do Ya Love Me (6.8) Julie's proposal song
I've Never Been to Me (1.11) Edie sings this at karaoke
What's Love Got to do With It (2.14) This plays at Susan's wedding
Theme from New York, New York (1.11) Susan sings this at karaoke
Down at the Ol' Five and Dime (1.11) Julie and her friends sing this at karaoke
There Was an Old Lady Who Swallowed a Fly (5.24) Dave, Susan, and MJ sing this in the car

Looking Glass - Brandy (You're a Fine Girl) (6.11) Tom sings this during physical therapy
Sleigh Ride (3.8) Andrew puts this music on while Bree writes her Christmas cards
Three Times a Lady (7.5) Lynette says Bree is "three times not a lady"
Jingle Bells (3.8) This is playing while Bree writes her Christmas cards
We've Only Just Begun (6.1) This song is in the order of service card for Susan and Mike's wedding
Angels We Have Heard on High (3.10) This plays at the Christmas party
Three Times a Lady (6.20) This is guessed at charades
Over the Rainbow (7.23) Karen says "Judy" is a little "over the rainbow"
Amazing Grace (8.17) Renee sings this at Mike's funeral
There's No Business like Show Business (8.3) Lynette sings this loudly
Here I Am (Come and Take Me) - Susan sings this while she is waiting for Mike (1.10)
Water Lady (Panihari) - this is playing at Lynette's yoga class (1.12)
Someone Like You - this is playing at the diner (1.13)
Me Against the World - playing at John's apartment (1.13)
Do the Damn Thing - plays at the dance (1.13)
Bittersweet - plays during Lynette and Tom's dinner (1.14)
Hear on the Radio - plays when Bree goes to visit John (1.15)
Reason is Treason - plays at Zac's party (1.15)
I Don't Want to Know (If You Don't Want Me) - plays at Zac's party (1.15)
Caribbean Queen (No More Love On the Run) - plays at the bar (1.16)
Ain't Nobody Like You - Nurse Heisel listens to this (8.17)
Set It Off - plays in Andrew's car (8.17)
Our Love Is Here To Stay (3.2) Bree and Orson's first dance
Shut Up (3.2) Plays when Austin is fixing his motorbike

Bridal March (3.2) Plays when Bree walks down the aisle
Proud Mary (3.3) Lynette is listening to this in the car
Non, je ne regrette rien (3.4) Plays while Susan and Ian are in bed
It's My Party (4.2) Bree refers to this song, in a play-on-words
Love On The Run (7.2) Plays in the bar when Bree goes to find Keith
Vision is Clear (7.3) Plays when Renee is going home with Keith
Start All Over Again (7.5) Emma sings this at the piano for her performance
One Less Bell to Answer (7.9) Renee is crying on the couch to this song
Finding Something To Do (8.2) Can be heard at the party
Headspace (8.2) Playing at the party
We Don't Need Love Songs (8.11) Plays in the bar
Wonderful, Wonderful (8.23) Plays while Karen is dying
Vision Is Clear (8.18) Plays at Andrew's party
Dreaming Out Loud (8.13) Plays at the bar
Clock On The Wall (8.12) Plays at the bar
American Dream (8.11) Bree talks to Bradley
Hotel California (5.6) The band is letting Orson sing lead vocal on this song
Free Bird (5.8) Mike says if Ann Shilling requests this song, then the band will do it
YMCA (8.14) Gaby says "it's fun to stay at the YMCA"

Literature Referenced in the Show

Books

AIDS and HIV Infection (3.10) This can be seen in Orson's office

Affirmation for Women Who Do Too Much (2.20) Susan gives this to Edie to help get over her break up with Karl

Antony and Cleopatra (6.14) Tom and Lynette's counselor is in this play

Ants In My Picnic Basket
> (2.4) Susan signs copies of this in a flashback with Lonny
>
> (3.20) Susan signs copies of this at Travers' birthday party
>
> (5.14) Susan gives this book to the school principal

Beowulf (6.7) Denise jokes about this book

Cinderella (3.9) Susan is compared to her, when she loses her shoe at the start of the episode

Crime and Punishment (6.7) Susan is reading this in jail

Dante's Inferno (8.4) Andre Zeller painted a series based on this

Dinosaur Book (5.1) Susan asks MJ if he has packed this to read with Mike

Doctor Porcupine (8.4) One of Susan's bestselling children's books

Down Home Cooking with Mrs Van De Kamp (6.17, 6.19) Bree's second cookbook

Eagle State College of the Arts Course Catalog (8.4) Susan is reading this

English to Mandarin Dictionary (5.24) Tom buys this with his other college supplies

Fairview High School Yearbook (6.7) Mike is looking through this

Fishing with the Pro (3.22) Mrs Simms is reading this when Edie visits
Flashpoint (7.19) Chris Cavanaugh, the keynote speaker is said to have authored this
Frankenstein (4.6) Adam comes to the Halloween party dressed as Frankenstein's monster
Goldilocks and the Three Bears 3.16 Carlos calls Tom 'Foldilocks'
Goodnight Moon (6.1) Lynette was happy to be done with this book
Grapes of Wrath (7.4) Gaby said Carmen went all "Grapes of Wrath"
Great Romances of our Time (1.4) This is sitting on Gaby's porch table
Harriet the Spy (3.11) The Scavo kids give Kayla this
Harry Potter (7.17) Mike read this to MJ
Harvey The Flying Turtle (1.10) Lynette reads this to her kids
Hausfrau (6.5) Gaby calls Heidi Bremmers friends her "Hausfrau cronies"
Heal Through Counseling (8.4) Lynette reads out this book title
Hope in a Bottle (2.20) Susan gives this to Edie to help get over her break up with Karl
How the Grinch Stole Christmas! (6.10) Karen references going 'all Grinch'
I, Claudius (3.14) Bree says Orson's mother is straight out of this book
India on Fifty Rupees a Day (8.21) Tom is going to give McGuiness this book
It's Not You (2.20) Susan gives this to Edie to help get over her break up with Karl
Kama Sutra (7.9) Karen was reading this and it led to Roy being injured
Kids First: The Big Book of Seperation (8.4) Lynette is reading this at the start of the episode
King Arthur and His Knights of the Round Table (7.7) Susan says she painted this on MJ's wall

Little Red Riding Hood (1.6) Lynette is on the committee for the school production of this
Live to Love: Letting Go of Grief (2.20) Susan gives this to Edie to help get over her break up with Karl
Lord of the Flies (8.2) Toph says the party is a Lord of the Flies situation
Madame Bovary (1.7, 5.6) The book club is reading this
Marmaduke (8.15) Roy said if Marmaduke ate his pillow, he'd shoot him
Mary Poppins (2.4) Tom said that Parker really locked into the whole Mary Poppins thing.

Meet Dick and Jane (8.8) Gaby says the art show is like a Dick and Jane book

Men and Postpartum: The Bitter Seed (7.2) Tom comes home with this

Moby Dick (6.14) Robin is reading this at the bar

Mrs. Van de Kamp's Old Fashioned Cooking
         (4.17, 5.1, 5.2, 5.4, 5.6, 5.7, 5.8, 5.9, 5.13, 5.14, 5.18, 6.4, 6.5)
         This is referenced frequently during Bree's catering career

Much Ado About Nothing (2.11) This is on Zach's homeschool reading list
Murder in March (5.4) Orson is reading this in bed
Murder on the Orient Express (8.4) Lynette picks this book up
Paradise Lost (8.3) Susan is reading this at the park
Paul Revere's Ride by Henry Wadsworth Longfellow (1.17) The school kids are rehearsing this
Pearl Buck (6.12) The Reverend says he read this
Peter Pan
    (5.22) Tom calls Bill Peter Pan
    (7.9) Tom and Lynette have sex "in front of Peter Pan"
Poof! Goes the Princess (5.21) Juanita is reading this in bed
Pride and Prejudice (6.9) Julie is reading this at the library
Road to Reconnection (8.4) Lynette reads out this book title
Robin Hood (4.1) Barcliff Academy do this play at school
Romance Novel (7.4)
Romeo and Juliet (6.20) Eddie's mother calls him Romeo
Secrets of Italian Cooking (6.7) Bree is reading this at the end of the episode
Skippy Bedelle (6.6) Juanita is reading this for homeschool
Stepford Wives (1.1) Andrew says Bree is the one always running for the mayor of Stepford
The Art of Moving On (2.20) Susan gives this to Edie to help get over her break up
The Bible
    (1.8) Bree is reading this as the episode opens
    (3.9) Vern asks Gaby to "be their Moses", Gaby says the modeling parties were "this side of Gomorrah"
    (3.21) Victor quotes Luke 12:48
    (4.11) The beginning narration talks about families leaving with their bibles
    (6.5) The hotel maid tells Bree there is a bible in the nightstand. The bible can also be seen in the draw at the end of the episode

(6.8) Gaby refers to the parting of the Red Sea
(6.12) Bree questions if the minister is quoting from this
(7.12) The minister and Bree have a 'verse-off'.
(7.16) Bree compares herself with the character of Job

The Case of the Missing Man (2.20) Bree is reading this in bed
The Fairview Homeschooling Workbook (6.7) Juanita throws this on the floor
The Family Bed (4.8) Bree has been reading this
The Fish in Shoes (7.9) Grace is reading this
The Fun of Homeschooling (1.5) Lynette is reading this
The Generic Drug Manual (4.7) Bree looks up Mike's pill in this
The Help (8.9) The receptionist at rehab is reading this
The Old Man and the Sea (2.11) This is on Zach's homeschool reading list
The Pearl (2.11)This is on Zach's homeschool reading list
The Shawshank Redemption (6.6) Gabrielle says, "What is this? Shawshank Elementary?"
Tips for Surviving a Nuclear Attack book (8.6) Jasper is reading this
To Kill a Mockingbird (8.3) Susan is shocked Carlos hasn't read this
Treating the Criminally Insane (5.7) Dr Hellyer's best-selling book
War and Peace (6.14) Robin says she almost killed a guy with this
Willy Wonka (6.18) Gaby calls Susan Willy Wonka
Winnie the Pooh (8.15) Susan suggests a Winnie the Pooh mural for the wall
Women Who Can't Love (2.20) Susan gives this to Edie to help get over her break up with Karl
Yellow Pages (4.8) Lynette is looking through this
Your Husband's Banging Somebody (fictional) (8.4) Renee says this book title is for Lynette

Magazines

Dazzle (1.18) Susan is reading this at the salon
Playboy Magazine (5.3) Tom says he has to stash his old copies of this
Dream Magazine
    (1.18) Sophie is reading this at the salon
    (2.12) Gaby is reading this on the porch
Trendy (1.18) Gaby is reading this at the table
Stylit (1.4) This is on Lynette's coffee table
Body Movin (6.1) The pregnant woman is reading this in the waiting room
Magazine (title can't be seen) 2.22 - Gaby is reading this in bed
Newsview (1.4) This is on Lynette's coffee table
Tomorrow's Bride (1.4) This is on Lynette's coffee table
The National Informer (1.4) This is on Lynette's coffee table
Travel
    (1.4) This is sitting on Gaby's porch table
    (3.23) Stella is reading this
Perkins College Catalogue (2.21) Peter brings this over for Andrew
Modern Mother
    (6.4) Bree is on the cover of this, on her office wall
    (6.16) Bree is on the cover of this, and it hangs in her office
Woman's Circle
    (3.2) Gaby is reading this at the hospital
    (3.5) Gaby is reading this in bed
Vogue
    (6.17) Gaby was even on the cover
    6.22 Gaby shows Patrick a photo of her from Vogue
    (7.4) Gaby said she used to sneak copies of this out of her aunt's salon
    (8.3) Renee tells Jenny to go and read the latest vogue
    (3.8) The girl scout reads this from her list

(3.13) Zac read the issue of this that Gaby was in
Hot Rods Today (3.4) Andrew is reading this
Sports Illustrated
    (5.10) Mike says Katherine could be on the cover of this
    (6.17) Because of Gabrielle, Heidi Klum didn't get to be on the cover of this
Menopause Monthly (5.10) Susan says Katherine could be on the cover of this
Sports Action (3.5) Carlos is reading this on the porch
Muscle Mover Mag (7.2) Tom is reading this in bed
Redbook (3.8) The girl scout reads this from her list
Eagle State College of the Arts Course Catalog (8.4) Susan is reading this
Glamor (3.8) The girl scout reads this from her list
Independent Woman
    (1.19) Gaby is reading this in bed
    (3.18) Gaby is reading this at the rally
    (4.14) A lady at Susan's birth class is reading this
Parents Weekly
    (1.21) Lynette is reading this on the couch
    (4.11) Susan is reading this
    (1.4) This is on Lynette's coffee table
    (5.12) Edie holds this up and makes Susan guess which month it is
Rods: Special Issue (2.19) This is in Andrew's porn box
Leather Daddies in Love (2.19) This is in Andrew's porn box
Tales from Space (3.8) Parker is reading this
Superman No.13 (Nov–Dec 1941) 3.11 Carlos calls Gaby's boyfriend 'Jimmy Olsen'
Tres Chic - Gaby is reading this (3.12)
Female Workplace
    (3.12) This is on the table that Lynette and Tom are kissing on
    (6.4) Bree is on the cover of this, on her office wall

Cosmopolitan - Zac read the issue of this that Gaby was in (3.13)
Golf Survey (8.20) Tom's magazine which was sent to Lynette
Cat Fancy (3.14) Gaby says she now has to subscribe to this
Travel Times
    (3.12) This is on the table that Lynette and Tom are kissing on
    (4.7) Gaby has this when she says a month in Rio would be so romantic
    (4.15) Gaby is reading this
Bio (4.3) Stella is reading this
Living Times (4.7) Stella is reading this at the kitchen table
Women's Day (5.4) This magazine is running an article about Bree's new cookbook
The New Christian Reader (5.7) Bree reads an advance review for her cookbook from this
Sword Monger Magazine (5.12) Edie holds this up and makes Susan guess which month it is)
Commotion
    (4.8) Gaby throws this on the bed
    (5.21) Juanita is looking at this in Gaby's room
    (7.15) There is a poster of this at Gaby's old school
    (6.1) Lynette picks this up in the waiting room
Big Cans (6.1) Parker is reading this
The Fairview Enquirer (8.21) The two ladies are reading this in the supermarket
Fairview Home and Garden
    (6.5) Bree is reading this in the motel room
    (6.19) Gaby is holding this at Bob and Lee's
    (7.1) Gaby received Bree's magazine and kept it
Bridal Quarterly (6.16) Susan brings this to Karen
Marie Claire (8.5) Gaby was reading this during her hot stone massage
Paris Match - Gaby said she was on the cover of this (3.12)

Sport Today (5.24) Mike is reading this at the airport
News Today (6.2) Lynette is reading this in the waiting room
Econ Weekly (6.17) Angie is reading this at the modeling agency
Prink (6.17) Gaby is reading this at the modeling agency
Psychiatry Monthly (7.14) Susan is reading this at the hospital

Book Reviews

Mrs. Van de Kamp's Old Fashioned Cooking

Mrs. Van De Kamp's colorful stories of her upbringing show her upstanding values — but her recipes are sinfully delicious!

985743-00492
By Bree Van de Kamp
Fairview Publishers, 250pp, $29.99

HALO METER
4 OUT OF 5 HALOS

From the practical to the inspirational, from quiet suppers for two to dinner parties for ten, Mrs. Van de Kamp's Old Fashioned Cooking has options for every meal and every cook, with family-pleasing classics, new fare, and twists on both. Whether you're looking for an easy weeknight dinner such as Tuna Steaks with Mint Sauce or a sophisticated hors d'oeuvre like Prosciutto Crostini and Fresh Figs with Gorgonzola or a rich dessert like the Ultimate Malted Brownie Sundae, Mrs. Van de Kamp's Old Fashioned Cooking provides excellent choices across 22 categories. In addition to recipes for all-time favorites such as Lasagne Bolognese, Chicken Soup with Dumplings, the Best Onion Rings, and Apple Pie with Cheddar Crust, you will find helpful how-to photographs that demystify preparations for piecrust, gnocchi, soufflés, and more. Here, too, are cooking tips and techniques, nutritional information for healthy choices, comprehensive pantry and equipment glossaries, menu ideas, and a resource guide for finding ingredients.

With stunning color photography and an easy-to-follow, comprehensive format, this new volume is a must-have reference that will become a loved and oft-used favorite of every home cook.

A friend just gave me Mrs. Van de Kamp's Old Fashioned Cooking. It's by none other than Bree Van de Kamp, herself, and it's not that he didn't like it; he's moving and just doesn't feel like hauling it to Europe! He knows I'll give it a good home.

I find that I can't be as upset with her as many of the Epsilon reviewers are because they seem to think the demands that you follow her every suggestion. Hello! Is any one home? That's all they are ... suggestions. If you are too busy raising a family or whatever, just take her with a grain of salt and wait until the kids leave and then do all of her cute stuff.

I'm still not over being slightly angry with Bree for being tangled up with that awful K-Mart/Blue Light free BS! When I had Blue Light they were constantly pushing Bree's stuff so I can understand that it was a business tie-in: K-Mart carries her bedding (and God only knows what else) that I have never made the effort to see. Now we are all watching her stock market scandal with bated breath ... some pro, some con.

Let's start with the cover. It's turquoise and pea-green slipcover with a picture of the Goddess grinning at me over a crock of something I suspect she would say was "a good thing". Inside I am told that the more than 1,600 recipes are the culmination of all the work and collecting of recipes she has done since 1982. I'm told I can learn to make Bree's most popular hors d'oeuvre - Shrimp Wrapped in Snow Peas. I think I'll skip that one.

I like my shrimp steamed with the shells on and then chilled. My sure visits for the Great Circus Parade every July and we talk and eat our way through two pounds of those delicious crustaceans. There's just a big bowl of shrimp, lemon wedges and some fresh cocktail sauce made with fresh horseradish; we get caught up on a year?s family gossip.

The first section is simply called the BASICS, as it should be; how nice to start off with something a lot of us overlook. Does everyone really know how to make

CONTINUED PAGE 40

> *In addition to recipes for all-time favorites... you will find helpful how-to photos that demystify (more complex) preparations*

Newspapers

The Fairview Herald
    (1.17) Carlos is reading this
    (2.10) This can be seen sticking out of Curtis' bag
    (3.18) The Fairview Herald sponsors the mayoral debate
    (3.19) The Fairview Herald runs a story on Victor and Gaby
    (3.21) Tom is reading this in bed
    (4.12) Everyone is reading this at the end of the episode
    (4.13) Tom is reading this at the start of then episode
    (7.1) Carlos is reading this at the end of the episode
    (7.8) Carlos is reading this in the kitchen
    (7.11) Renee is reading this on her porch
    (7.19) Susan hands Paul his newspapers
    (8.6) Carlos is reading this
    (8.18)8 Bree is holding this when she talks to Renee and Ben
    (6.19) everyone is reading this at the start of the episode
    (6.2) Bob is reading this on the porch
    (6.4) Bree is on the cover of this, on her office wall
    (6.14) A review in this called the therapist's performance "incandescent"

Clarion Examiner (4.12) Wayne is looking through this
The Daily Independent Banner Times (4.12) Wayne is looking through this
The Times (5.14) They put Bree's book on their bestseller list
Sports Banner Times (4.12) Wayne is looking through this
The New York Times (4.17) Someone from this newspaper is on the phone for Bree
Mount Pleasant Gazette (5.17) Edie does her research at this newspaper
The Plainview Herald (3.16) They said Victor had an "ingratiating wit" and "trustworthy smile"

The Wall Street Financial (3.19) Victor is reading this at the breakfast table

The Miracle Worker
New Caterer Bree Van de Kamp Works Magic With Food and Decor

BY ERIK CARLSON
HERALD STAFF WRITER

Bree Van De Kamp was born Bree Helen Kostyra on August 3, 1941 in New Jersey. She was the first daughter of Eddie and Bree Kostyra. She was born to a large middle class family of Polish heritage. She has a older brother, Eddie. She also has 4 other siblings.

When she was born, her family lived in an apartment in a two-family home. They bought a house in Nutley, New Jersey when Bree was three years old. It was a busy household with six kids. Bree's mother cooked and sewed clothes for the family. She saved money by making the childrens' clothing. Bree's parents believed in a strong work ethic.

Bree's mother taught her how to cook. They had large Christmas

Bree van de Kamp, above, has taken the Fairview social scene by storm, creating a perfect blend of professionalism and warmth rarely seen from a catering service.

The Fairview Herald
STYLE

Modern Day Wonder

Bree Van de Kamp's Test Kitchen Surprises, Amazes, Amuses

BY MICHAEL REINHART
HERALD STAFF WRITER

Since its founding 6 years ago, Mrs. Van de Kamp's Kitchen has been based in suburban Fairview. As the company has grown, so has its territory: a TV studio, one floor of a former industrial warehouse, and then a second, for merchandising, the Internet division, the prop house, photo studios, even the food department, which quickly outgrew its original kitchen. Throughout these buildings, each office becomes an individual laboratory, helping to shape and inspire the staff's endeavors. To celebrate the connection between the personal and the professional, Bree asked renowned photographer Kim Hix to document the spaces that spark our creativity.

Bree's company in Fairview is a work in progress. She purchased the 153-acre property in 2000 and, since then, has been gradually restoring and renovating the property, making new additions and refurbishing existing buildings.

Once called Sycamore Farms, Bree's new property was first settled in 1764 and is known locally, today, as Cantitoe Corners. (Cantitoe was the wife of an Indian chief named Katonah who lived in the region in the 1700s.)

Bree's new home is more like a small village, with a series of houses and out-buildings dotting the expansive grounds. Bree resides in the 1925 farmhouse (the Winter House), shown above – a three-story abode fronted by a long porch and dormer windows on the third level. Adjacent to the farmhouse is the property's original abode, a 1776 Colonial house, known as the Summer House. There is also a nearby tenant's cottage, where her daughter, Alexis, lives when she is visiting.

Incidentally, this is the property where Bree served her five months of house arrest – a time she describes as "hideous" since her movements on the property were severely restricted.

With rolling fields and swaying sycamore trees, the property is one of the finest in the region, adjacent to the home of fashion designer Ralph Lauren.

The town of Fairview could best be described as 'gentrified English country' with rustic stone walls and winding roads driven by men behind the wheels of antique roadsters. The women spend their days in the gardens

See Kitchen, F3

(Above) WHERE THE MAGIC HAPPENS
Bree Van de Kamp's Test Kitchen is filled with sensible design choices, much like her work.
HERALD PHOTOS BY KIM HIX

(Above) OFFICE WORKPLACE THE EPITOMY OF STYLE SENSIBILITY
Bree Van de Kamp's Test Kitchen is filled with sensible design choices, much like her work.

Poetry

First They Came… (4.5) Lee recites this
Do Not Stand at my Grave and Weep (4.10) Mrs. McCluskey recites this
Walt Whitman (5.2) - Porter says he likes Walt Whitman's poetry
Emily Dickinson (5.2) - Lynette says she kicks Walt Whitman's ass
William Butler Yeats, The Lover Tells of the Rose in His Heart (5.2) Preston sends this to lynette
Serenity Prayer (2.20) This is recited in the AA meeting
(7.17) This is recited in the AA meeting

Authors

Agatha Christie (5.6) Karen calls her sister "Miss Marple"
Robert Frost - Karl said Orson's Bimbo will use this as a coaster (5.22)
Jackie Collins (6.6) Susan said Katherine's bathroom was like "a bad Jackie Collins novel"
The Bronte Sisters (8.11) Bree calls Renee's breasts "The Bronte sisters"
Edward Albee (3.9) Orson asks how many more "Edward Albee dinners" they will have to sit through
Mickey Spillane (6.21) Bree says the measures sound like a Mickey Spillane novel

Books Related to the Show

Eva's Kitchen" Cooking with Love for Family and Friends, 2011,
Eva Longoria

Burnt Toast: And Other Philosophies of Life, 2006,
Teri Hatcher

A Practical Handbook for the Boyfriend: For Every Guy Who Wants to Be One/For Every Girl Who Wants to Build One, 2007,
Felicity Huffman

Desperate Housewives: Behind Closed Doors, 2005,
Touchstone Television

Reading Desperate Housewives: Beyond the Picket Fence, 2006,
Janet McCabe and Kim Akass

The Desperate Housewives Cookbook, 2006,
Christopher Styler and Scott Tobis

The Unofficial Cookbook of Desperate Housewives, 2021,
Johny Bomer

Welcome to Wisteria Lane: On America's Favorite Desperate Housewives, 2006,
Leah Wilson

Desperate Housewives of the Bible, 2007,
Robert Strand

Not-So-Desperate: Fantasy, Fact and Faith on Wisteria Lane, 2006, Shawnthea Monroe

Illnesses Referenced in the Show

Acid Reflux (3.10, 3.20)
Acne (2.5, 3.8)
Alcoholism (2.17, 3.17, 6.8)
Allergies (2.15, 4.9, 8.6)
Angina (3.8, 8.22)
Anti Social Behaviour (6.13)
Arthritis (1.19, 3.22, 4.6, 6.23)
Asthma (4.9, 6.16)
Attention Deficit Disorder (1.4, 1.6, 1.8
Bipolar Disorder (6.13)
Black Eye (5.9)
Blindness (4.10, 5.10)
Blisters (6.8)
Blood Blisters (8.4)
Boils (7.16)
Borderline Personality Disorder (1.6)
Botulism
Breast Cancer (1.12)
Broken Bones (1.7, 2.2, 2.16, 2.23, 5.9, 5.22, 6.3, 7.7, 7.23, 8.4)
Broken Crown (3.8)
Bulimia (6.17)
Bunions (1.19, 7.6, 8.18)
Burns (5.9)
Cancer (1.12, 2.14, 4.6, 4.7, 4.8, 4.12, 4.17, 5.5, 5.16, 5.19, 5.22, 5.24, 6.10, 6.16, 6.18, 7.12, 7.22, 8.1, 8.4, 8.5, 8.6, 8.14, 8.15, 8.16)
Cardiac Arrest (3.10)
Cardiac Event (2.9)
Chicken Pox (2.12, 6.16)
Chlamydia (3.4)
Cholera (7.6)
Cirrhosis (5.11)

Cleft Palate (3.16)
Color Blindness (3.23)
Coma (1.8, 1.10)
Common Cold (6.8)
Concussion (3.14, 3.19, 4.8)
Crabs (3.4, 4.4)
Cracked Ribs (5.9)
Cut (2.2)
Defomed Kidney (7.6))
Delusion (6.13)
Dementia (5.3, 5.5, 5.20, 7.6)
Depression (1.6, 1.8, 1.19, 5.10, 6.6, 7.3, 7.7)
Deviated Septum (7.5)
Diabetes (4.6, 7.15, 7.22)
Dislocated finger (6.22)
Double Pneumonia (6.20)
Drug Addiction (4.7, 4.8)
Dysentery (4.11)
Ebola (2.12)
E Coli (8.12)
Eating Disorder (4.3)
Egg Allergy (2.10)
Electrical shock (5.5)
Embolism (1.11)
Epilepsy (4.6)
Enlarged Prostate (8.20)
Erectile Dysfunction (3.14)
First Degree Burn (8.18)
Flu (5.2)
Fractured Rib (3.19)
Gallstones (6.22)
Glaucoma (3.2)
Gonorrhea (5.10, 5.20)
Gout (6.13)
Gunshot Wound (1.14, 3.7, 3.8)
Head Lice (1.16)

Headache (1.8)
Heart Attack (1.10, 1.11, 1.22, 2.3, 5.13, 5.19, 5.20, 6.10, 7.21, 8.14)
Hemorrhage (4.9)
Hemorrhoids (2.5)
Hepatitis (3.6, 8.2)
Herpes (4.4, 6.12, 8.19)
High Blood Pressure (8.22)
High Cholesterol (6.14)
Hodgkin's Lymphoma (3.22)
Hypertension (4.6)
Hypothermia (4.8)
Impetigo (3.2)
Indigestion (7.7)
Inner Ear Balance Disorder (3.5)
Kleptomania (7.6)
Leprosy (8.1)
Liver Spot (8.2)
Measles (1.16)
Menopause (4.1, 7.7)
Migraine (4.1)
Miscarriage (2.7, 6.10)
Mutilation (2.12)
Nausea (2.5)
Neck Spasm (8.8)
Nervous Breakdown (6.4, 6.13)
Neutropenia (4.5)
Night Sweats (3.10)
Non-Hodgkin's Lymphoma (3.22, 4.1, 4.2, 4.3,
Nose bleed (1.18)
Pericarditis (1.11)
Placental Abruption (6.10)
Placental Disruption (4.3)
Postpartum Depression (7.2)
Prostate Cancer (4.7)
Psychological Depression (3.10)

Pulled hamstring (5.9)
Restless Leg Syndrome (7.15)
Rheumatoid Arthritis (7.15)
Ruptured Disc (3.17)
Ruptured Kidney (7.6)
Salmonella (8.23)
Schizophrenia (1.4)
Sex Addict (2.18)
Sexsomnia (7.2)
Shingles (6.4)
Skin tag (1.19)
Smoke Inhalation (5.9)
Snoring (5.9)
Sprain (3.4, 4.9, 5.4)
Strep Throat (2.12)
Stomach Cramps (3.10)
Stroke (3.1, 3.15, 5.11, 5.12)
Sunburn (1.4, 4.12)
Syphilis (4.4)
Tetanus (4.5)
The Clap/Gonorrhea (4.4)
Third Nipple (4.6)
Thrown out back (2.1)
Ticks (4.13)
Tooth Decay (5.4)
Twisted Ankle (3.21)
Visual Impairment (8.9)
Wandering Spleen (2.12, 2.13, 2.14)
Weak Heart (5.23)
Webbed Feet (4.6)
Weight Problem (5.1)
Wounds (5.9)
Yeast Infection (3.10)
Yellow Fever (2.10)
Yellow Jacket Stings (2.22)

Sports and Games Referenced in the Show

Aerobics (8.5)
Age of Empire III (4.15)
Air Hockey (1.23)
Ballet (6.3, 6.15, 7.14, 8.5)
Baseball (1.13, 1.16, 1.18, 1.22, 2.3, 2.19, 3.4, 3.13, 3.21, 4.10, 4.13, 5.1, 5.2, 5.3, 5.5, 5.6, 5.10, 5.20, 5.21, 7.1, 7.12, 7.13, 7.15, 7.18, 7.20, 7.21, 7.22, 8.1, 8.8, 8.11, 8.14, 8.17)
Baseball Video Game (3.21)
Basketball (1.11, 2.1, 2.18, 3.16, 3.17, 3.20, 4.13, 6.14, 7.1, 7.7, 8.1, 8.13, 8.22, 8.23)
Beer Pong (3.22)
Bike riding (1.3, 1.5, 1.18, 2.2, 2.7, 4.3, 5.4)
Bodybuilding (4.14)
Bowling (1.7, 2.2, 2.11, 3.4, 6.8, 5.10, 6.22)
Boxing (3.12)
Bridge (1.22, 5.5)
Camping (3.3, 5.15, 6.16, 6.22, 7.21)
Cannonball (1.1, 2.23)
Capoeira (5.3)
Cards (2.18)
Cha Cha (5.3)
Charades (4.3, 6.20)
Checkers (5.3, 6.21)
Cheerleading (2.16, 2.20, 2.21, 2.23, 3.13, 3.17, 4.4, 5.2, 6.7, 6.8, 6.20)
Chess (2.14, 2.18)
Cribbage (5.20)
Cricket (3.18, 8.11)
Croquet (1.20)
Dance (5.10, 5.11)
Darts (3.6)
Diving (2.23)

Fantasy Football (4.4)
Fishing (4.8, 5.2, 5.21, 5.18, 5.23, 5.24, 6.22, 8.14)
Football (1.5, 2.1, 1.18, 2.13, 2.14, 2.16, 2.20, 3.9, 3.10, 3.16, 4.1, 4.3, 4.16, 5.2, 5.3, 5.10, 5.21, 6.18, 7.7, 7.8, 8.1, 84, 8.17)
Frisbee (1.4, 1.13, 3.5, 4.3)
Golf (1.9, 1.13, 1.16, 2.2, 2.4, 2.6, 2.11, 2.12, 2.16, 2.23, 3.1, 3.2, 3.4, 3.22, 4.5, 5.12, 5.15, 5.21, 7.1, 7.2, 7.7, 7.14, 7.17, 7.20, 7.22, 8.1, 8.15, 8.22)
Hangman (6.12)
Hearts (1.22)
Hide and Seek (5.24)
Hiking (2.18, 3.21, 4.15, 5.18, 8.5, 8.18)
Hockey (1.15)
Hopscotch (5.17)
Horseback Riding (2.6)
How Big is Mommy's Tummy (4.4)
Hunting (1.8, 4.57.18)
Jazz (6.3)
Jogging (1.3, 1.7, 2.2, 6.20, 6.21, 7.2, 7.4, 7.11)
Jousting (3.20)
Jump Rope (1.18, 4.3, 6.18)
Jumping Jacks (1.5)
Karate (8.19)
Kickboxing (8.2, 8.13)
Knot Tying (1.8)
Kung Fu (5.3)
Lap Dancing (6.14)
Lego (3.7, 3.18)
Mahjong (1.22, 4.5)
Marco Polo (8.2)
Martial Arts (8.15)
Mechanical Bull (1.7, 5.4)
Mega Monopoly (8.2)
Mini Golf (1.22)
Model Aeroplanes (3.17)
Monopoly (7.17, 8.2)

Mountain Climbing (5.3)
Olympics (3.5, 5.10)
Ouija (7.15)
Paintball (7.16)
Pilates (1.9, 2.18, 4.5, 5.16, 8.5, 8.16)
Pinata (3.1)
Pinball (3.9)
Pole Dancing (6.12, 8.2)
Polo (3.18)
Pool (5.9, 5.19, 5.20)
Poker (1.3, 1.6, 1.12, 1.16, 1.18, 2.9, 2.14, 3.10, 3.16, 3.18, 3.20, 4.15, 4.17, 5.1, 5.13, 5.17, 5.21, 6.9, 7.3, 7.4, 7.14, 7.18, 8.1, 8.2, 8.5, 8.7, 8.8, 8.23)
Puzzle (1.5, 1.22, 3.20, 4.16)
Queen City Rum (4.2)
Relays (1.5)
Roller skating (2.2, 2.16, 4.3)
Rollerblading (7.7)
Rugby (7.1)
Running (1.5, 1.7, 3.7, 3.8, 4.2, 5.19, 6.21, 8.1)
Russian Roulette (2.23)
Sailing (7.8)
Salsa Dancing (1.22, 2.5, 3.13, 7.19, 8.18)
Scooter (1.18)
Scouts (1.8)
Scrabble (7.13, 8.16)
Self-Defence (6.9)
Shooting (1.1, 1.12, 4.16)
Shuffleboard (7.12)
Skateboarding (4.2)
Ski (2.5, 4.14, 5.22, 6.22, 7.2)
Skiing (8.18)
Sled Pulling (1.5)
Slot Machine (7.18)
Smash the Bottle (8.12)
Snap (3.16)

Soccer (1.1, 1.2, 1.3, 1.4, 1.5, 1.7, 1.19, 2.16, 2.21, 2.24, 5.2, 5.3, 5.22, 6.16, 7.8, 7.12, 8.5,8.6, 8.8, 8.21)
Softball (5.17, 8.19)
Spades (7.22)
Spin Class (8.4)
Stretching (6.16)
Swimming (1.1, 1.3, 1.9, 2.4, 2.23, 3.8, 3.9, 3.10, 4.16, 6.11, 7.19, 8.17)
T-ball (5.7)
Tango (3.12, 3.18, 8.23)
Tap Dancing (5.21, 7.16)
Tennis (1.1, 1.3, 1.6, 1.13, 1.14, 1.17, 1.19, 3.18, 3.23, 4.11, 5.16, 5.22, 6.16, 7.16)
Track (1.3)
Train set (3.8)
Treadmill (2.23)
Video Game (3.11, 5.6)
Waltz (8.23)
Water Aerobics (4.5, 7.13)
Water Polo (3.18)
Weightlifting (3.12)
Wrestling (1.4, 5.4)
Yachting (1.5)
Yoga (1.1, 1.4, 1.5, 1.12, 2.6, 2.8, 2.12, 2.19, 3.2, 4.6, 5.14, 6.11, 7.19, 8.2, 8.3, 8.12)
Yoga Meditation (1.12)
Zombie Video Game (4.5)
Zumba (8.2)

Pets and Animals

Bongo (1.1. 1.2, 1.8, 1.23, 2.1, 2,8)
Mr Whiskers (1.5, 2.11)
Fake Gopher (1.5)
Unnamed Bird (1.8)
'Iffy' Llama (1.16)
Patches (2.19)
Rat (2.2)
'Loyal Friend' (2.5)
Dog (2.14, 4.10, 7.9, 7.21)
Scavo Dog (2.19, 3.18, 8.14)
Pig (3.5)
Carolyn and harvey's dog (3.7)
Baxter (3.8)
Alma's Parrot (3.1)
Alma's Bird (3.13)
Toby (3.15, 4.9, 4.14, 5.2, 5.5,
Fenway (3.21)
Raphael (4.4)
Travers' Turtle (3.17)
Frog (4.6, 6.23)
Scruffles (4.6)
Seahorse (4.7)
Roxy (4.13, 4.15, 4.16, 4.17)
Seeing Eye Monkey (4.13)
Coco (5.15)
Taffy (5.15)
Munchy (5.15)
Dog (5.17)
Monkey (6.5)
Beth's Fish (7.2)
Cupcake (7.23)
Spider Monkey (8.2)

Bruce (8.12)
Penny's Goldfish (8.7)
Rufus (8.16)
Juanita's Gerbil (8.12)
Chipmunk (7.15)
Sparky (7.6)

Oakridge Animal Groups

MATHS
- Leopards
- Chipumnks
- Giraffes

READING
- Otters
- Penguins
- Seals

Charades Teams (4.3)

Gaby (Captain)
- Orson
- Mike
- Bree
- Victor
- Adam

Susan (Captain)
- Carlos
- Edie
- Tom
- Katherine
- Lynette (the charades ninja)

Bree and Rex Control Words (1.14)

- Philadelphia
- Boise
- Palestine

SUBURBIA IS A BATTLEGROUND

EAGLE STATE, FAIRVIEW & WISTERIA LANE

Fairview
Eagle State
00057

Very few television show settings have received the same level of attention that has been given to Wisteria Lane, since the release of *Desperate Housewives* in 2004. This widespread discussion in newspapers, magazines, blogs, and online is understandable. Wisteria Lane, on the surface, appears to be the perfect place to live, which makes for the perfect juxtaposition with the 'desperate', complicated lives of the housewives who inhabit the homes on Wisteria lane. The picture perfect houses look almost too quaint to be real, a motif which surely finds its inspiration in the representation of small town life in films such as *It's a Wonderful Life* and *Stepford Wives.* According to American Cinematographer; "The centrepiece of the show, both physically and dramatically, is," the "rendering of the housewives' suburban Wisteria Lane neighbor-hood, which over the course of three seasons has grown to encompass 36 standing sets on the Universal Studios lot. Many of the show's interiors…are spread across six soundstages, but the bulk of the ground-floor sets are attached to the facades on the studio's 1,500'-long Colonial Street…Normally you just shoot the facades, then all the interiors are onstage…but here we're actu-ally able to look out the window and see the neighbors. As such, the neighborhood of Wisteria Lane really has a personality. It's like another character on the show.' The broad, winding lane with its well maintained grass and white picket fences takes on a life of its own in the show, demonstrated by the show's open from the high-angled shot of the lane, to the final tour through the lane and all those who died on it, in the series finale.

The set for Wisteria Lane is located within Universal studios Hollywood, and is referred to as 'Colonial Street'. Colonial Street has been used for many other films and television shows including *Gremlins, Buffy the Vampire Slayer, Ghost Whisperer,* and *Alfred Hitchcock Presents.* In addition, music video clips such as Nelly's *Dilemma,* and Micahel Buble's It's *a Beautiful Day* are filmed on the lane.. During the eight season run of *Desperate Housewives,* Colonial Street underwent some significant changes. This included removing large buildings and facades such as the colonial mansion seen in *Casper,* and the church seen on *Murder She Wrote.* These changes were necessary to make room for Edie's house and Wisteria Park. After *Desperate Housewives,* the set underwent further changes to remove the Wisteria Lane look, so that Colonial Street could be used in other productions.

The houses on Wisteria Lane were built prior to 1980, as that was when Karen McClusky moved into her home. The style of the homes suggest that they were built during the 1940s or 1950s. Surrounding stress include Hibiscus Circle, Hydrangea Circle, Cypress Lane, and Freshview Drive.

Fairview is the small, fictional city, in which Wisteria Lane, and *Desperate Housewives,* is set. Fairview sits within the "Eagle State", as shown by the vehicle number plates on the show. Throughout the series, and particularly in the beginning, the neighbourhood, and the lane is presented as a symbol of the idyllic suburban lifestyle that was associated with television in the 1950s. While the show does not disclose the precise location of the town of Fairview, there is some helpful information that is provided throughout the show's eight seasons:

- In 3.4 we are told that Fairview was founded in 1871 by Edward Sibley, who was known to be a bootlegger,

womanizer, and horse thief. Fairview sits within the fictional Eagle State, and is home to Wisteria Lane.
- Fairview is potentially one of the more southern states, as we never see any cold, wintery weather to suggest a northern or New England setting.
- In addition, the violent tornado in 4.9 indicates that it could sit within Tornado Alley.
- Since there are two major lakes mentioned in the show (Rockwater and Torch), it can be assumed that Fairview sits within driving distance to hilly, mountainous terrain.
- From mail sent within the show, we know that the zip code for Wisteria Lane is 00057, which is actually the zip code for Maccarese, Italy.
- In 2.5, Lonnie tells Susan that his family are "up in Minnesota", which suggests that Fairview, and the Eagle State are south of Minnesota.
- In 1.23, Felicia who is working as a nurse in Utah, says that she has family "way out in Fairview", which suggests that Fairview and Utah are significantly far away from each other
- Mentions of Purdue and Notre Dame University suggest that Fairview may be located in the Midwest
- Several residents of Wisteria Lane have moved from Chicago, including the Applewhite's and Mayfair's. In reality, there is a Fairview in Illinois.
- In 8.21, the seal in the courtroom is dated 1876. The only state to be admitted to the union in 1876 is Colorado.

The Houses of Wisteria Lane

#4344

- This house was used only once during the show's run, in Season 2.
- Lisa Sidment lives there with her son.

#4345

- This house was seen only once during the series, in Season 5.

#4346

- In Season 2 this house was owned by Sharon Shesin whose son was injured by the Scavo children.
- In Season 5 Mona Clarke lived there with her family.

#4347

- Ida Greenberg lives here until her death in Season 4, when Karen McCluskey moves in briefly.
- From Season 6 onwards Mitzi Kinsky lives there.
- Mike's Map shows that Garry Morris lives here with his wife

#4348

- This is Rose Kemper's house from Seasons 1 to 5.
- In Season 5 and 6 Mona Clark lives here.

#4349

- Carlos and Gabrielle Solis live at #4349 until the last episode of the series, when they move to Beverly Hills.
- In Season 4 they have two children, Juanita and Celia who become permanent residents of the home until the end of the show.
- In Seasons 2 and 3 Xiao-Mei also lived here, and in Season 4 Carlos and Gaby took in a boarder by the name of Ellie.
- In Seasons 5 and 6 the Solis house also becomes home to Ana Solis.
- The house was repainted from a muted mustard yellow to a brighter yellow in Season 6. In the 7th Season, windows were also added to the garage door.
- In Season 8, the living room was redecorated as part of Alejandro's murder story arc, and was painted grey with new curtains and carpet.

- In Season 8, Roy Bender temporarily lives there.
- Aside from the entry area and the living/dining room, all inside shots of the Solis house are filmed on a soundstage.
- Backyard scenes are filmed on a lot in the San Fernando Valley, California.

#4350

- Martha Huber lives here in Season 1, and then Edie moves in after her house is burned down.
- Martha Huber moved into the house in the 1980s with her husband Mason who died in 1990.
- After Martha's death, Felicia Tilman lives in the house until she leaves.
- In Seasons 4 and 5 Mr and Mrs. Addams live in the house until they sell it
- In Season 5 the house has been painted a pale yellow, and Bree buys the house for Andrew and Alex who live there until Season 7 when Alex leaves Andrew.
- Andrew has moved out by mid-Season 8, by which time the house has been restored to its original green colour.

#4351

- In Season 1 Edwin Mullins lives here with his wife.
- Mr Mullins was a taxidermist who kept a spare key to Mrs McCluskey's house
- Bree had a key to their home
- Mr and Mrs Mullins move out near the end of the season due to everything that has happened in the lane over the past year
- According to Mike's map, Trent and Debra Nelson live here
- In Season 2 the Applewhite's live here.
- In Season 3 Alma Hodge lives here briefly until her death
- In Season 4 it is purchased by Bob and Lee, but they sell it to Paul Young in Season 7.
- In Season 7 Bob and Lee adopt Jenny, and she becomes a resident of this home
- Apart from the kitchen and dining, all interior scenes in this house are filmed on a soundstage

- This house was used as 1313 Mockingbird Lane in *The Munsters*

#4352

- From the pilot, this is Paul and Mary Alice Young's house.
- The Young's moved into the house in 1990 with their son Zach
- In Season 3 the house is bought by Arthur Shepherd after Paul is arrested
- After the tornado in Season 4 this house underwent some changes on the outside, including removing the archway in the front yard.
- In Seasons 4 and 5 Mrs Hudson lives here
- In Season 5 Edie and Dave buy the house and rent it to Mike Delfino.
- In Season 6 Nick and Angie Bolen move in.
- In Season 7 Paul rebought the house to turn it into a halfway house for former convicts
- Kitchen, bedroom, and bathroom scenes in this house are filmed on a soundstage

- Parts of the house were used for filming interior scenes of Bree's house in Season 1
- Backyard scenes are filmed in a house in the San Gabriel Valley, California
- This house has been used in several other projects including *The United States of Tara*

#4353

- This is Susan Meyer's house throughout the series.
- Susan and Karl moved into the house in 1992 with their daughter Julie
- This house was burned down by Edie, but rebuilt almost identically
- Mike moves in during the show, and Julie moves out.
- In Season 1 Sophie Bremmer moves in briefly
- In 4.16, Susan gives birth to MJ and he becomes a resident of the home until the end of the series
- In Season 6 Robin Gallagher moves in briefly
- During Season 7, Paul lives in the house before Susan and Mike move back into it briefly in Season 8.
- In Season 8 Julie moves back in when she is pregnant
- At the end of the series, Susan sells the house and we meet Jennifer who, with her husband Steve, will be moving into the house.

- Interior shots of the family rooms, dining room, bedrooms and bathroom are filmed on a soundstage

#4354

- Bree and Rex Van de Kamp live here in Season 1.
- Rex and Bree moved into the home in 1994 with their children Andrew and Danielle
- In Season 1 Rex moves out and back in until his death
- In Season 2 Bree kicks Andrew out
- In Season 3 Bree marries Orson and he moves in, along with his mother Gloria, for part of the season.
- In Season 3 Danielle moves out briefly when she is sent to live in a convent during her pregnancy
- When Danielle has her baby, Benjamin Hodge becomes the newest resident of the home until Danielle takes him back in a Season 5 flashback
- In Season 5, the garage on Bree's property has been converted into a test kitchen for Bree and Katherine's catering company.

- Katherine briefly moves in to help Bree with her alcohol addiction
- In Season 7 Keith moves in
- In Season 8 Renee Perry moves in to go on suicide watch for Bree
- Above the kitchen, on the second floor are the offices. At the end of the show, Bree moves to Kentucky with her husband Tripp.
- Bree's house has no interior for shooting scenes. This space is used as cast and crew restrooms
- Bree's backyard is one of only two on the lane to have backyards

#4355

- This is the Scavo house throughout the show, until Tom and Lynette move to New York at the end of the series.
- Tom and Lynette moved in in 1997 where they grew their family to include Porter, Preston, Parker, Penny and Paige
- Tom's daughter Kayla moves in Season 3, and moves out again in Season 4
- In Seasons 3 and 4, Lynette's mother Stella moves in
- Eddie Orlofsky moves in during Season 6, before turning himself into the police
- The Scavo's backyard is one of only two on the lane to have backyards
- The Scavo house is just a shell with no interior. All interior shots are filmed on a soundstage

#4356

- This is referred to as the Simms house at times, as Lillian Simms lived there for several years preceding the show until she moved to a retirement home
- After Katherine divorced Wayne she moved in with Lillian along with her daughter Dylan
- Dylan died in this house in 1995
- This was Mike's house for the first three seasons of the show
- In Season 3 Carlos moves in with Mike
- Mike moves in with Susan, leaving the house with Carlos
- Katherine moves back in Season 4 with her husband Adam and the new 'Dylan', and Lillian is brought back home to die
- In Season 5 moves back in to live with Katherine
- In Season 6 Mike moves out to marry Susan

- It was remodeled between Seasons 3 and 4 with the wall around the staircase being removed and the walls being re-wallpapered.
- In Season 7 it was the Graham house, before Paul Young purchases it in Beth's name
- Felicia Tilman moved in after Beth's death.
- At the start of Season 8, Ben Faulkner moves in.
- The house has a complete first floor interior. Upstairs scenes are shot on a soundstage
- Four characters died in the house over the course of Season 4: Dylan Davis, Lillian Simms, Ellie Leonard, Wayne Davis

#4358

- This is the home of Karen McCluskey throughout the show.
- Gilbert McCluskey lived in the house until his death, after which his body was stored in Karen's freezer
- After the tornado in Season 4 the house was destroyed and rebuilt.
- In Season 6, Roy Bender moves in with Karen.
- Porter and Preston Scavo move in as boarders briefly in 8.14
- Orson Hodge moves in briefly after his accident
- This house is the only one on the Colonial Street set to have a complete interior - first and second floor

#4360

- In Season 2 Mona Clark lives here, though in Seasons 5 and 6 she is living at #4348.
- In Season 3 there is a blonde woman living there, and in 4.2 a woman with black hair.
- Karen McCluskey reports a man washing a pig on the lawn of this property in Season 3.
- In Season 7 it is revealed that Mr Scully lives here
- Before *Desperate Housewives*, this property was home to retail store facades and a school.

#4362

- This is Edie's house until her death in Season 5.
- Edie lived in this house with her husband Umberto Rothwell before the start of the series
- The house was burned down in the pilot and rebuilt.
- Karl Mayer moves in with Edie in Season 2
- Edie's nephew Austin McCann moves in, in Season 3
- In Season 3 Carlos moves in with Edie, and they have temporary custody of Edie's son Travers
- In Season 5 it is shown that Edie rented to a man named Raymond who lived in the house between the Seasons 4 and 5 time jump
- In Season 5 Dave Dash/Williams and Edie move back
- After Edie's death, Dave lives there alone until he is institutionalized
- In the webisodes *Another Desperate Housewife* that take place during Season 6, Stephanie lives in the house

with her husband Lance. After Lance's death, it is presumed that Stephanie moved out.
- In Season 7, Renee Perry lives in the house.
- For reasons that are unclear, in 7.8 and the series finale, the numbers on Renee's house are 4359.
- It is presumed that after Ben and Renee's wedding Ben moves into this house
- Before *Desperate Housewives*, this property was a church facade, most famously seen in *Murder, She Wrote*.
- The house was yellow before it burned down, and is pink after.
- The house has a complete downstairs interior Second floor scenes are filmed on a soundstage
- This is the only house on the lane to have running water

Mapping Wisteria Lane

Mike's Map

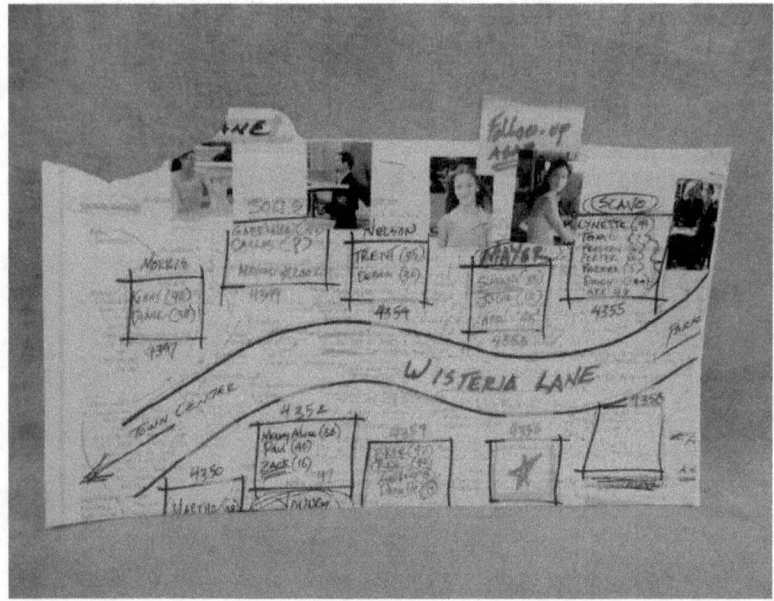

In 1.2 a map of the street can be seen in Mike's home. This map covers the main characters' houses, but doesn't show the whole lane as seen in later seasons, including the cul-de-sac. There are some notable differences between Mike's map, and the official map produced by the show:

- Two of the house numbers have changed. The Applewhite house is noted as 4354 (rather than 4351), and Bree's is 4359 (rather than 4354).

- The Applewhite house is known to be home to the Mullins in Season 1, though Mike's map shows that Trent and Debra Nelson live there
- #4347 is shown to be home to Gary Morris and his wife who are 42 and 38, rather than Ida Greenberg

Behind Closed Doors Map

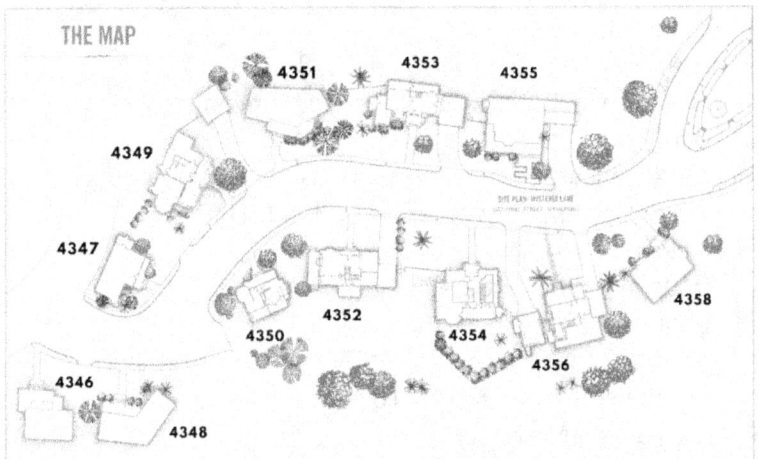

A Map of Wisteria Lane is featured in the Season 1 companion book of the show *Desperate Housewives: Behind Closed Doors* (2005). A simplified version of this map can be seen above.

This map doesn't label the McCluskey house, Ida Greenberg's or Rose Kemper's house. It also doesn't cover the lower part of the cul de sac where Edie's house sits.

Both Mike's map, and this one start at 4346 Wisteria Lane, indicating that 1-4345 do not exist.

Businesses, Organisations and Brands

24-Hour Liquor Store (3.9)
5th Avenue Beauty Salon (4.12)
Ad Agency (5.17)
Adult Bookstore (3.9)
Afternoon Preschool (5.4)
Air Brazil (5.22)
Airport (1.13, 3.3, 3.11, 5.24, 7.18, 8.9)
Al Kaminsky Certified Public Accountant (4.3)
Alcoholics Anonymous (2.16, 2.18, 7.18, 8.18)
All-American Girls League (4.10)
Alvin Portsmith Divorce Mediation (3.1)
Amtech (7.19)
Amusement Park (8.13)
Andare (3.17)
Antique Shop (2.6, 6.15)
Antique store on Pearl St. (6.6)
Athena You Move (1.22)
Atlantic City Hotel (2.22)
Attenborough High School (2.5)
Auto Club (1.12, 2.12)
B&B (7.22)
Baby Land (2.8)
Bail Bondsman (3.9)
Balfor and Barasso (2.13)
Balta Flowers (3.18)
Bank (7.2, 7.14)
Bakery (7.8)
Bar (1.16, 7.2, 8.9)
Barcliff Academy (1.5, 1.16, 3.8, 3.18)
Beacon St Pharmacy (1.11, 1.13, 1.19, 1.20, 2.3, 2.8, 2.24)
Beauty by Vern (3.9, 3.10, 3.13)

Beecher Academy (5.19)
Bergman Gallery (8.8)
Betty Ford Clinic (3.18)
Bicks Aerial Banners (6.10)
Bierlich Construction Co. (4.10)
Big Top Burger (8.21)
Bonny Briars (4.7)
Book Store (1.5)
Boot Camp (5.14)
Boston Ridgegate Mental Hospital (5.24)
Boy Scouts (1.6)
Braille School (4.16)
Bree Catering Company (4.17, 5.1, 5.2, 5.6, 5.7, 5.8, 5.15, 5.17, 5.18, 5.19, 5.21, 6.3, 6.4, 6.7, 6.8, 6.16, 6.17, 6.19, 6.22, 7.15, 7.16, 7.21)
Brettanion Hotel (2.6)
Burger Barn (5.22)
Burnham Fox (3.4)
Cafe (6.5, 7.11, 8.2)
Calgary Rodeo (2.18)
Camp Hennessy (1.17, 1.18, 1.19, 2.4, 2.10)
Camp Kickapoo (7.6)
Candle Making place (7.22)
Cappy's (3.5)
Car Dealer (7.17)
Global Venture Group (5.11, 5.15, 5.16, 5.17, 5.18, 6.8, 6.9, 6.10, 6.12, 6.21, 7.17, 8.8, 8.16)
Casino by the Airport (7.18)
Carnival (4.15)
Carpet Store (8.12)
Catering by Katherine (4.13)
Catholic Church (2.10, 2.13, 4.8, 4.11, 5.16, 7.4)
Catholic School (6.8)
Cemetery (1.17, 2.5, 3.16, 5.10, 7.18)
Cenn and Simmons (2.1)
Cheerleading Camp (2.23)

Chez Naomi (2.15, 3.10, 3.16, 6.17, 7.3, 8.5)
Chicago Lumber Yard (2.23)
Chicago Memorial Hospital (4.5)
Chicago Metropolitan Police (2.5)
Child Protective Services (4.16)
Children's Hospital (3.9)
Chinese Restaurant (3.1)
Chiropractor (7.11)
Christies (5.17)
Church (7.13)
Circus (5.2)
City Hall (5.22)
City Trust & Savings Bank (3.16, 4.4)
City of Fairview Chamber of Commerce (3.5, 4.4, 5.15)
City of Fairview Coroner (2.11)
Cliffside Cable (1.4, 1.16, 4.5)
Clothing Store (4.15)
Community Center (5.11, 8.18)
Coney Island Beach Club (7.8)
Continental Overnight (8.3, 8.6)
Cornell University (5.3)
Cucina (3.16, 3.18)
Cumberly's (8.18, 8.19, 8.20, 8.23)
Cyprus Office Products (1.7)
Dance Club (6.1)
David Bradley Law (2.4
Department Store (5.9, 6.1)
Department of Motor Vehicles (2.1)
Department of Water and Power (5.6)
Diner (1.13, 1.15, 2.14, 2.24, 3.10, 3.16, 4.13, 6.9)
Disneyland (1.3)
District Attorney (5.11)
Doctors without Borders (3.16, 3.21)
Doctor's Office (2.10)
Dorset Security Company (2.1)
Double Ds Gentleman's Club (6.12, 6.14, 6.17, 6.19, 6.21, 8.2)

Dr Henry Gable Office (7.6)
Dr. Oakley, PhD (4.14)
Drama Camp (3.4)
Dress Shop (3.21)
Dry Cleaners (6.16)
Duke University (7.7)
Durber Advertising (5.4)
ESPN (7.23)
Eagle State College of the Arts (8.4)
Eagle State University (6.13)
Edie Williams Realty (5.11)
El Royale Motel (3.5)
Elegant Chocolate Fountains (3.23)
Elks Lodge (3.9)
Ellen's Screen Printing and Promotional Products (5.17)
Ellsburg Hotel (1.22)
Elm Ridge Mental Hospital (3.10)
Ernie's Bar (5.11)
Excellence One Day Shipping (4.5)
Expert Alteration (6.9)
Fairview Childbirth Center (8.21)
Fairview County Courthouse (1.10, 1.16, 2.15, 5.10, 5.22, 8.21, 8.22)
Fairview Health Centre (6.13)
Fairview Mental Health Specialists (6.13)
Fairview 1st Baptist Church (2.3, 4.6)
Fairview Adventure Scouts (1.8)
Fairview Behavioral (6.15, 6.16)
Fairview Bus Terminal (6.23)
Fairview Chamber of Commerce (1.6, 5,4, 5.18)
Fairview Construction Inc. (1.17)
Fairview Country Club (1.10, 1.13, 1.16, 1.19, 2.23, 3.6, 5.2, 5.6, 5.7, 5.11, 6.8)
Fairview County Jail (2.3, 2.4, 2.5, 2.8, 2.23, 3.11, 3.12, 3.14, 5.5, 5.19, 5.23)
Fairview Elementary School (1.4, 6.6)

Fairview Farmers Market (2.6, 3.18)
Fairview Fertility Clinic (2.21)
Fairview Field (3.4)
Fairview Fire Department (5.8)
Fairview Food Van (2.4
Fairview Garden Club (5.20)
Fairview General Hospital (6.10)
Fairview Guide Dog Kennel (4.13)
Fairview High (4.13, 7.14)
Fairview Home and Garden (7.1)
Fairview Homeowners Association (4.5)
Fairview Mall (1.5, 1.11, 2.16, 2.24, 4.11, 4.13, 4.16, 5.1, 5.9, 6.2, 6.5, 6.21, 7.1, 7.18, 8.7, 8.19)
Fairview Market (8.2)
Fairview Meadows Psychiatric Hospital (2.22, 2.23)
Fairview Memorial Hospital (1.1, 1.2, 1.10, 1.12, 1.14, 2.9, 2.10, 2.13, 3.1, 3.2, 3.3, 3.4, 3.5, 3.6, 3.9, 3.13, 3.14, 3.15, 3.16, 3.19, 3.22, 4.2, 4.3, 4.8, 4.9, 4.10, 4.14, 4.15, 4.16, 5.1, 5.4, 5.5, 5.6, 5.9, 5.20, 6.2, 6.4, 6.23, 7.1, 7.17)
Fairview Memorial Park (2.4
Fairview Motor Inn (7.13)
Fairview Movers (1.22, 8.23)
Fairview Outlet Mall (6.18)
Fairview Pharmacy (4.8, 4.9, 4.12, 6.14)
Fairview Police (1.4, 1.5, 1.7, 1.8, 2.1, 2.10, 2.11, 2.12, 2.16, 2.23, 3.2, 3.4, 3.7, 3.9, 3.10, 3.12, 3.14, 3.15, 4.8, 4.10, 4.12, 4.13, 4.15, 4.16, 4.17, 5.5, 5.8, 5.10, 5.12, 5.20, 5.21, 5.23, 5.24, 6.10, 7.1, 7.15, 7.20, 7.21, 7.23, 8.10, 8.15, 8.16, 8.17, 8.18, 8.18, 8.19)
Fairview Police Impound Lot (5.23)
Fairview Post Office (4.12, 4.16, 6.3)
Fairview Presbyterian Church: Women's Auxiliary (4.11, 8.12)
Fairview Presbyterian Church (4.11, 4.16, 5.24)
Fairview Realty (1.22, 2.1, 3.1, 3.5, 3.7, 3.9, 3.12, 4.4, 4.15)
Fairview Towers (4.15)
Fairview Town Council (4.6)

Fairview You Move (1.19, 2.23. 2.24)
Field's Market (3.7, 3.9)
Fire Department (2.22, 6.11)
First Methodist Church (2.1)
Fish and Disco (3.5)
Fitness Center (8.4)
Foxy Brown (8.12)
Fortune 400 (3.12)
Fortune 500 (7.19)
Foundation to Protect Wild Horses (2.10)
Frames Parts (5.17)
French Bistro (4.11)
French Restaurant (7.2, 7.5)
Gable and Thompson Construction (1.22, 2.1)
Gabrielle's Closet (8.23)
Gas 'n' Gulp (2.16, 2.21)
Gaultier (3.17)
Gay Bar (7.22)
Geist Realty (2.11)
Gennaro's (8.2)
Gerard's (7.15)
Germani Vineyard (1.8)
Girl Scouts (7.21)
Global Cable News (2.5)
Global Group Venture (5.17, 5.22, 6.3, 6.4)
Goodwill (8.19)
Gospel Church by the airport (4.11)
Gourmet Americana (5.2)
Grandpa Slim's (4.7)
Granville Field (4.10)
Greater Fairview Chamber of Commerce (5.21)
Green Grocer (4.16)
Greenbriar Country Day School (5.8)
Greenwood Rehabilitation Centre (4.9, 4.11)
Group Home (8.19)
Gun City (4.6)

Gustave on Main (8.12)
Hadassah Women's Zionist Organization of America (3.19)
Hairdresser (5.16, 8.12)
Halls of Justice (1.23)
Halston (1.9)
Happy Housekeepers! (6.7)
Haunted House (7.6)
Harvard Medical School (4.1)
Harvard University (4.7)
Heart's Desire (5.7, 5.16, 7.5)
Heisler Beer (5.11)
Hilltop Insurance (5.7)
Hinterland (2.9)
Hodge General Dentistry (3.10)
Homeless Shelter (5.22)
Homeowner's Association (7.9)
Hooters (2.20)
Hospital (1.12, 5,10, 5.12, 6.9, 6.11, 6.21, 7.2, 7.3, 7.11, 7.12, 7.13, 7.16, 7.18, 7.19, 7.21, 8.2, 8.14, 8.15, 8.23)
Hotel (1.3, 2.15, 2.23, 4.11, 5.12, 6.16, 7.11, 7.15, 8.2)
Howell's Rent-a-Truck (2.23, 2.24, 8.23)
Howe's Market (6.21)
Hudson's Market (6.21)
Hydrangea Circle Homeowners Association (7.10)
Huffington promotions (2.22)
Infinity Airlines (3.3, 5.24, 8.9)
International Monetary Fund (8.11)
Internal Revenue Service (4.2, 4.6)
Italian Restaurant (7.22)
Jefferson Elementary (6.12)
Jewelers (5.15)
Jewelry and Watch Repair (6.9)
Jewelry Store (8.17)
Jewelry Store on Maple (6.7)
Jimmy Choo (5.13)
John Rowland's Restaurant (6.3)

Johnson Real Estate Inc (7.6)
Johnson Realty (8.22)
John's Gardening Business (3.3)
Justice Department (1.11)
Justice of the Peace (5.12)
KQRY (6.11)
KQRY Eyewitness News (3.3, 3.21)
Kentucky State Legislature (8.23)
Kerwin Jewelers (2.23, 3.16, 3.21)
Kindergarten (5.4)
KYAP (7.15)
La Tarola Grill (4.15)
Lacroix (3.17)
Lamaze (4.14)
Lang Enterprises (3.16)
Las Brisas Spa (1.18)
Le Petite Fleur (1.14)
Leonardo's Bar and Grill (2.15)
Lexington Hotel (5.15)
Library (6.9)
Lingerie Store (1.5)
Liquor Store (5.16)
Little Boutique on Lake Street that Chuck's wife owns (7.23)
Little Broadway Theatre (3.21)
Louisville City Council (8.23)
Macy's (3.14, 4.1)
Madame Kim's Day Spa (3.20)
Malone Enterprises (6.7)
Mama Rego's (3.6)
Mario's (8.10)
Martinelli's (6.8)
Maserati of Fairview (1.20)
Mask shop, Venice (5.22)
Mary Beth's Frozen Custard (8.18)
McArthur High School (5.2)
McMay's (2.17)

Meadowbrook (3.1)
Medical Examiner's Office (2.5)
Meditation Seminar (8.3)
Mexican Restaurant (2.2)
Midtown Dental (7.9)
Mike Delfino Plumbing (3.5)
Mini Golf World (1.22)
Miss Charlotte's Doll Academy (7.11, 7.12, 7.13)
Misty Spring (2.10, 2.19, 2.23)
Mitchell and Kerns (1.22)
Modeling Agency ' The House that Bulimia Built' (6.17)
Modeling Agency (1.11)
Mood Lounge (1.5)
Moroni Movers (1.23)
Morris Technologies (7.17, 7.19, 7.20)
Motel (2.24, 3.11, 7.9, 8.13, 8.17, 8.19)
Motel by the interstate (5.12, 6.3, 6.5)
Motor Lodge (1.3)
Mount Pleasant Gazette (5.17)
Mount Pleasant Wedding Chapel (2.14)
Movie Cinema (1.7, 2.19, 3.18, 5.10, 5.12)
Mr Francois (4.13)
Muir & Hunt (2.5)
Murray's Tavern (8.11, 8.1, 8.13)
Nail Salon (4.16)
National Rifle Association (1.1, 1.5, 8.20)
Neighbourhood Watch (1.5, 2.8, 2.10, 6.2, 6.5)
Night Club (5.11, 5.19)
Nighttime Necessities (1.21)
Nords (1.9)
Northwestern (5.17)
Nursing Home (3.8, 3.9, 6.5)
O'Donnell's (2.5)
Oakridge Open House (7.21)
Oakridge Parent's Council (7.21, 8.5)

Oakridge School (5.14, 5.15, 5.17, 5.18, 5.21, 6.12, 6.13, 6.18, 7.6, 7.21, 7.23, 8.4, 8.13)
Office of Dr Heller and Philip Lybrand, PhD (5.11)
Offices of Adoption Attorney Eugene Beale Esq (2.16, 3.21)
Open Mic Restaurant (1.11)
Overeaters Anonymous (8.18)
Oyster Bar (3.21)
O'Brien's (5.2)
Parcher and Murphy (2.1, 2.3, 2.5, 2.6, 2.9, 2.13, 2.14, 2.16, 2.17, 2.18, 2.20, 2.21, 3.8, 3.13, 5.4)
Pancake Castle (7.8)
Parent Teacher Association (1.7, 1.15, 8.4)
Park (5.11, 6.21)
Parsons Christian Academy (2.20)
Passention's Pizza (5.5)
Perchik Modeling Academy (1.7)
Perkins College (2.21)
Perry Scavo Designs (7.7, 7.13, 8.8, 8.12)
Pet Shop (7.7, 8.2)
Peterson Advertising (1.20)
Petting Zoo (1.16)
Piccolino's (6.7)
Pick your own apple orchard (7.22)
Pizza world (6.23)
Pizza/Arcade (1.23)
Polar Fresh Mints (2.16)
Police Academy (8.2)
Police Station (8.9)
Pool (4.9)
Post office (3.18)
Presbyterian Church (7.12, 7.20)
President's Council of Economic Advisors (7.19)
Pretzel Vendor (6.5)
Price Warehouse (4.12, 5.11)
Princess Dress Store (5.1)
Princeton University (4.17)

Printers (4.13)
Prison (6.10, 7.1, 7.7, 7.8, 7.9, 7.17, 8.2)
Prudey's Feed Store (2.8, 2.9)
Psychiatric facility (5.12)
Purdue University (3.8)
Quickcast Cable (8.18)
Rancho Mi Familiar (3.13)
Reagan Library (7.3)
Red Panda (4.15)
Renee and Lynette Decorating Firm (7.20)
Rent a Reptile (3.20)
Restaurant (1.6, 1.21, 3.8, 3.11, 3.12, 5.15, 6.6, 6.17, 7.4, 7.9, 7.11, 7.16, 8.3, 8.11, 8.12, 8.13, 8.19, 8.20)
Restaurant on Third Street (5.9)
Retirement Home (5.12)
Retirement Village (7.13)
Rib Joint (6.10)
Rick's (4.12, 4.13)
Rockwater Bank and Trust (3.2, 5.16)
Rockwater Lake Termite Control (2.19)
Romanian Orphanage (4.17)
Rotary club (3.17)
Royal Kailua Spa and Resort (7.21)
Russells Delivery Moving and Storage (2.23, 2.24)
Russian Embassy (6.19)
Sacred Heart Chapel (6.11)
Sacred Heart Hospital (1.8, 1.17, 1.18, 2.16, 2.17)
Safe-T-Move (3.21)
Sakura (8.5)
Salon (2.15)
Salutations Home (3.16)
Santa Maria's Church (7.3)
Sardi's (6.2)
Scavo's Pizzeria (3.6, 3.11, 3.12, 3.13, 3.14, 3.15, 3.16, 3.17, 3.18, 3.20, 3.21, 3.22, 4.1, 4.8, 4.12, 4.13, 4.16, 5.1, 5.3, 5.5, 5.6, 5.10, 5.14, 5.15, 5.16, 7.20)

Schaefer Ambulance (4.4, 6.2, 6.10, 7.11)
Second Chance Community Correctional Center (7.9)
Seven Falls (4.12)
Sex Addicts Anonymous (2.18)
Shanghai Panda (5.17)
Shangri La Motel (6.1, 6.9, 6.10)
Shanta Yoga Center (1.12)
Sheffield School for Boys (3.10)
Shelter (3.11, 4.9)
Shooting Range (4.16)
Shorecrest Coach Bus Terminal (5.9)
Siesta King (1.14)
Silvercrest Juvenile Rehabilitation Center (1.6, 1.9, 2.20)
Silverfizz (5.2)
Sinclair Hotels (3.3, 4.5)
Sisters of Hope Convent (4.4)
Spa (7.14)
Social Services (1.2, 5.20)
Soulfood Place (3.20)
Soup Kitchen (8.5)
Soup Kitchen at St Malachi's (3.3)
St Timothy's Church (3.6)
St Ursula's School (6.8)
State Penitentiary (6.9)
Statewide Moving Crew (2.23, 4.4, 8.23)
Sterling Recovery Center (8.9, 8.10, 8.11, 8.12, 8.13, 8.16)
Stevens Properties (3.1)
Strip Club (6.9)
Summer Camp (3.18)
Sunny Pastures Retirement Home (3.22)
Sunset Garden Villas (4.5)
Supermarket (1.4, 1.5, 2.10, 3.8, 6.5, 6.16, 7.15, 8.23)
Susan Jewelry Business (7.1)
Swat (2.24)
Tailor's (6.5)
Tasty Treat (2.20)

Teleshore (5.6)
Temptation (2.17, 2.18)
Tennis Club (3.23)
The Art Institute (6.20)
The Ass Menagerie (6.12)
The Bennet Group (8.11)
The Brittannian Hotel (6.19)
The Brunswick Inn (5.15)
The Cancer Ward (8.6)
The Carlyle (8.15)
The Chocolate Box (5.17)
The Chuckle Zone (6.12)
The Civic Center (4.1)
The Coastguard (4.8)
The Coffee Cup (1.20, 5.1, 6.8, 6.8, 6.18, 6.19, 6.20, 6.21, 8.14)
The Community Center (1.19)
The Enchanted Florist (3.11, 3.13, 3.21, 4.12)
The Fairview Herald (1.17, 3.18, 3.21, 8.22)
The Fairview Junior League (2.9)
The Four Seasons (4.1)
The Frost Hotel (8.9, 8.21)
The Garden Center (4.6)
The Gardening Channel (3.3)
The Gardening Store on Euclid (8.8)
The Golf Course (3.22)
The Hammond Hospital (8.20)
The Hammond Library (8.20)
The Hammond Theatre (8.20)
The Hamper Dry Cleaning (3.21, 4.16)
The Jingle Bells (6.10)
The Ice Cream Man (1.19, 3.14)
The Lipstone Clinic (1.22)
The Loll Group (2.16)
The Morgue (4.8)
The Museum (4.11)

The Needle Exchange (4.3, 4.12)
The Neighbourhood Association (4.4)
The Oaks (3.22)
The Office of Dr. Samuel Heller Psychiatrist (5.7)
The Palm (5.14)
The Pancake House (3.3)
The Pancake Shack (1.18)
The Park (5.14)
The Plainview Herald (3.16)
The Rec/Youth Centre (3.8, 3.10)
The Rialto (1.4)
The Ritz (8.18)
The Rotary Club (6.19)
The Saddle Ranch (1.1, 1.7, 5.19)
The Senior Center (8.2)
The Smokehouse Lounge (7.5)
The Transvestite Bookstore (4.3)
The Traveller's Hotel Chain (1.22)
The Victorian Rose (6.6)
The Water Park (2.7)
The White Horse (5.7, 5.8, 5.11, 5.23)
Therapist Office (6.21)
Thomas Realty (8.11)
Tile Yard (8.8)
Topless Karaoke Tuesdays (6.12)
Topsy Turvey (1.4)
Town and Country Hardware (3.10, 3.21)
Town and Country Insurance (2.2)2
US Army (7.8, 7.15)
US Army Special Forces (7.10)
US Mail (2.5)
USCIS (6.19, 7.9)
Ungaro (3.17)
United States Citizenship and Immigration Services (5.22)
United States Environmental Protection Agency (5.3)
United States Postal Service (8.16)

University of Bucharest (6.7)
Utah Hospital (1.23)
Va Va Va Broom (7.1, 7.2, 7.3, 7.4, 7.5, 7., 7.21)
Vance Events Party Planning (3.2)
Vanover Medical Center (4.12)
Versace (5.24)
Veterinarian Office (5.1)
Video Store (5.10, 6.22)
Villa Foster (3.1)
W. T. Johnson's Hauling (3.3)
Waldorf University Law School (6.11)
Weight Loss Clinic (6.18)
Western Brothers Storage (5.22)
Westside Properties (2.11)
Wig shop (4.4)
Wisteria Lane Book Club (1.7, 7.23)
Witness Protection Program (6.10)
Women's Shelter (7.21)
Wooden Toy Maker Workshop (1.9)
Xpress Movers and Storage (2.23, 2.24)
X-Stasy Sex Swing (8.4)
Yale Divinity School (7.16)
Zimms (2.16, 2.17)
Zoo (5.10)

Events

10th Annual Wisteria Lane Blood Drive (2.12)
10th Annual Wisteria Lane Holiday Frolic (3.1)
4th July Barbecue (6.12)
AA Meetings (2.16, 2.17, 2,20, 7.17, 8.6)
Adam's Party (6.16)
Andrew Dinner Party (7.1)
Andrew and Mary Beth engagement party (8.18)
Anniversary Party (4.13)
Annual Yuletide Festival (6.10)
Art Shepherd Protest (3.10)
Aunt Connie Party (5.23)
Back to School Night (8.4)
Band Camp (4.11)
Battle of the Bands (5.7, 5.8)
Benjamin Katz's Bar Mitzvah (7 years from next Saturday) (5.3)
Black Eyed Peas Concert (7.4)
Bob and Lee Karaoke Party (5.20)
Bob and Lee's Halloween party (4.6)
Bob and Lee dinner party (6.13)
Bonsai Expo (1.20)
Book Club (1.7, 3.13)
Booty Burn Ballet (8.4)
Bradley Scott funeral (5.17)
Brandon's birthday party (6.9)
Braverman Bar Mitzvah (5.5)
Breakfast for the Garden Club (5.1)
Brees Baby Shower (4.4)
Bree's Dinner Party (1.3, 3.1, 5.10)
Bree's 'Shame on you for thinking my husband killed someone' dinner party (3.11)
Brunch at Bree's (7.16)
Brunch with Bree's family (6.14)

Carlos going away party (1.20)
Carlos birthday (6.22)
Catholic Mass (2.9)
Celia Solis' birthday party (5.7)
Charity Auction at Ted's Gallery (5.2)
Christie's Sea Auction (5.17)
Chuck funeral (8.10)
Church Bake Sale (8.12)
City of Fairview Chamber of Commerce Leadership Luncheon (4.4)
College party (6.6)
Conference in Washington (4.1)
Congratulations Carlos Party - vision (5.10)
Cooking Demonstration at the Mall (5.9)
Danny Bolen Birthday Party (6.4)
Daphne Bicks and Jeff Bicks anniversary (6.10)
Dental Innovator of the Year Award (5.22)
Dinner Dance (6.3)
Dylan Senior Recital (4.15, 4.16)
Economic Development Forum (4.1)
Edie's "Your Forgiven" Party (5.1)
Eli Scruggs Funeral (5.13)
Emily's Funeral (6.9)
Emma's Princess Party (5.1)
FV High Reunion (7.14)
Fairview Adventure Scouts Annual Fundraising Drive (3.7)
Fairview Book Launch of Mrs. Van de Kamp's Old Fashioned Cooking (5.14)
Fairview Chamber of Commerce Annual Dinner (3.5)
Fairview Chamber of Commerce Businesswoman of the Year (5.4)
Fairview High School History Fair (3.4)
Fairview Latino Businessman of the Year (5.21)
Fairview Elementary School production (6.6)
Fashion Show (7.19)

First Annual Sacred Heart Charity Fashion Show, "Painting the Town Rouge" (1.9, 5.22)
Founder's Day Ball (5.18)
Gaby's Annual Barbecue (7.23)
Garage Sale: featuring menswear and sporting equipment (3.4)
Garden Club Lunch (5.5)
Gin-of-the-Month Club (4.7)
Global Group Venture Christmas Party (6.4)
Gottlieb Bris (4.7)
Gun class (7.22)
Henderson Reunion (6.4)
Juanita birthday party (5.17, 6.5, 7.11)
Julie Welcome Home Party (6.5)
Jump Rope Competition (6.18)
Junior Prom (5.7)
Karen McCluskey's 70th birthday party (5.6)
Karen's 'I Survived Cancer' Party (6.18)
Karl 35th Birthday (6.9)
Karl Funeral (6.11)
Katherine and Mike Housewarming Party (5.16)
Kathryn's Housewarming Bbq (4.1)
Lee Dinner Party (7.18)
MJ Delfino's Sleepover (5.21)
Mary Alice Young Funeral (1.1)
Matt's Party on Crestview (4.2)
Mayoral Re-Election (7.10)
Meet the Teacher Night (5.4)
Meeting with the school board (4.1)
Michelle Downing's Party (5.2)
Mike and Susan anniversary (7.3, 7.16)
Mike and Susan vow renewal (7.16)
Mike's funeral (8.17)
Miss America (4.14)
Miss Snowflake Pageant (3.9, 3.10, 3.13)
Neighbourhood watch meeting (6.5)
Neil's Bar Mitzvah (2.19)

New Year's Eve Party (8.12)
Oakridge Fundraising Candy Drive (6.18)
Oakridge Parent Teacher Conferences (6.13)
One Village at a Time: Aid for Africa (2.10)
Oscars (5.21)
PTA Meeting (5.7, 8.4)
Penny birthday party (8.16)
Penny's Birthday (7.23)
Penny's Christmas Pageant (6.9)
Perchik Modeling Academy Summer Program (1.7)
Peter's Parents' 50th Anniversary (5.6)
Preston and Irina wedding (6.19)
Progressive Dinner Party (7.23)
Ray's Party (1.9)
Real Estate Convention (5.1)
Renee Bridal Shower (8.19)
Renee Spring Fling Party (7.17)
Renee and Ben Wedding (8.23)
Rex Funeral (2.1)
Rich Cohen's Bar Mitzvah (8.2)
Robyn's Cousin's Wedding (6.17)
Rotary Club Award Luncheon (3.17)
Scavo's After Hours Casino (5.1)
Scavo's Going Out of Business Sale (5.16)
Scavo's Grand Opening (3.15)
School dance (1.13)
Schwartzman Bar Mitzvah (6.21)
Second Grade Arbor Day Play (6.14)
Senior's Brunch (4.16)
Skinny Berry (8.3)
Steiner Bar Mitzvah (6.15)
Street Fair (3.13)
Sunday School (3.7)
Sunday School Pancake Breakfast (6.12)
Superbowl (5.21)
Susan 30th Birthday (6.9)

Susan and Karl 10th Anniversary (6.9)
Susan's Charade Night (4.3)
Susan's Traditional Welcome Dinner (1.2)
The 15th Annual Family Follies (2.3)
The Bake Sale (8.4)
The Barcliff Academy Fundraising Gala (4.1)
The Basketball Tournament (7.23)
The Boston Marathon (3.23)
The Christmas Carnival (8.2)
The Christmas Festival (8.16)
The Church Social (3.12)
The Donelly's Party (6.19)
The Fairview Herald Presents Decision Mayoral Race (3.18)
The Fairview Junior League Annual Fundraiser for the benefit of Fairview High School (2.9)
The Founder's Ball (4.12, 4.13)
The Groundbreaking for the New Civic Centre (4.1)
The Oakridge School Talent Show (7.16)
The Rialto Film Festival (1.4)
The Rotary Club Luncheon (6.19)
The Winter Gala (8.4)
Tom and Lynette anniversary (6.15, 8.8, 8.18)
Tony Awards (8.6)
Topher's party (1.16)
Travers Birthday Party (3.20)
Vanover Medical Center Benefit (4.12)
Victor's Mayoral Victory Party (3.21)
Vitale Anniversary Party (6.7)
Waldorf University Law School Graduation (6.11)
Walter and Shirely Lackey 50th Anniversary Party (6.14)
Wedding of Frank and Stella (7.13)
Wedding of Bree's clients (6.4)
Weisman Leadership Conference (7.19)
Fairview Hornets (1.15)
Church Raffle (6.21)
Summer Camp (6.21)

Spelling Bee (6.23)
Bruce Springsteen concert (7.1)
Wine Tasting (7.1)
Welcome Home Katherine party (6.15)

Advertising Accounts:
Black's Frozen Yoghurt (2.13)
Cosgrove's Revitalizing Serum (5.17)
Faraday Springs (1.22)
Hinterland (2.9)
Farm Fresh (2.13)
Galveston Jeweler's Account (2.14)
Hollister (1.22)
Traveler's Hotel Chain (1.22)
Halpern (1.20)
Kamarov (2.5, 2.6)
Necnet (1.22)
Oslo Candy (2.1)
Polish Sport (1.22)
Ponser Cheese (2.13)
Spotless Scrub (1.7)
The Bartlett Campaign (3.12)
The Boston Toy Company (2.21)

Places Mentioned on the Show

Asia - where Va Va Va Vroom is popular (7.6)
Africa - where Gaby wants Carlos to fly and nail "that nun" (2.11)
Argentina - where tangoing with a man and not having sexx with him is against the law (3.18)
Alendar - mayoral race results for this area can be seen on the television (3.21)
Alaska - where Sister Mary is being shipped off to (2.13)
- where Mike is (7.7)
- where Mike should have taken that job (7.6)
- where Orson and Bree were going to go on a cruise (8.15)
- where the weather is cold at this time of year (7.8)
- where Mike is thinking of taking a job (7.1)

Arizona - poster visible in Tom's office (1.20)
Atlanta - where Nick and Angie are going (6.23)
Atlantic City
- where Tom went on his last business trip (2.21)
- where Tom is heading (2.22)

Aspen - where Gaby wants a ski chalet (6.21)
- where Carlos is checking in, first thing in the morning (7.2)

Barbados - where Karl got Susan's sapphire earrings (6.6)
Bavaria - where Tom wanted some cheese from (6.17)
Belize - where Geoffrey took his dog (8.8)
Bermuda
- where Bree and Orson don't go on their honeymoon (3.3)
- where Mike and Katherine were talking about spending Christmas (5.10)

Boise - Bree and Rex's control word (1.14)

Boston - where Dave gets a string of calls from once a month (5.7)
- where Dr Sam Heller was from (5.23)

Botswana - where the church is sending a relief team (2.10)

Brazil - where Paul has been following the election results (2.15)

Bucharest - where Ivana has a PhD from the university (6.7)

Baltimore
- where Dylan is pushing Katherine to move to (5.12)
- where Katherine is looking for a house (4.15)
- where Roy knew a stripper named Cinnamon (7.8)

Bali - where Frank should want to be checking in on his salon from a beach (8.12)

Buckingham Palace - where Lady Catherine is the toast (7.11)

Chapman Woods (8.6)

Canada
- where Andrew could go (1.8)
- where Susan is going to kick Jackson's ass back to (5.21)
- there is a map of Canada on Penny's wall (8.11)
- where Jackson is going to be deported back to (5.22)

Cancun - where Carlos and Gaby broke the waterbed (1.3)

Cayman Islands
- where Carlos has a secret bank account (1.18)
- where carlos has 10 mil in an account (4.1, 4.6)

Chamonix - where Bradley has a chateau (2.5)

China
- where Xiao-Mei doesn't want to go back to (2.14)
- where Xiao-Mei's uncle will sell her (2.21)
- where Yao Lin is from (1.4)
- where Gaby is going to put Xiao-Mei on a plane to, on all fours in a rice patty (3.1)

Chinatown
- where Gaby promised to get Xiao-Mei an apartment (3.1)
- where Renee got her 'Woman Love Fluid' (8.6)

Caribbean - where Renee met most of her party friends (7.17)
Central Park - where Lynette and Tom bought an apartment overlooking (8.23)
Chapman Woods - where the bank owns the project now (8.1)
Coney Island - where Tom caught Renee in a towel (7.8)
Connecticut - where the Reverend Sikes grew up (7.16)
Croatia - where Lynette backpacked through (7.1)
Costa Rica - where Mrs Mcluskey got her flower pot (1.14)
Chicago
- where Adam had his tattoo removed (4.9)
- where Betty had packed up in the middle of the night before (2.23)
- where Betty's mother lives (2.12)
- where Bob and Lee's friend know about Adam's indiscretion (4.5)
- where Curtis Monroe is apparently from (2.12)
- where Katherine planned a few events (4.12)
- where Katherine took Dylan to a plastic surgeon (4.16)
- where Sylvia was one of Adam's patients (4.9)
- where the police received Betty's letter (2.5)
- where Anabel moved back to (1.20)
- where Tim Baker was sent to head up a new office (6.8)

Cleveland - where Carlos has to go tomorrow (5.13)
California - where Gaby and Carlos bought a mansion and argued happily ever after (8.23)
Denver - where Kimberly is from (7.15)
El Paso
- Carlos told Gaby his father left his mother for a waitress from here (1.5)
- where the mother of Gaby and Carlos' biological daughter lived (7.3)

England
- where Mrs. Mulberry went to take care of Spencer (2.4)
- where Virginia needs to go for two months (5.6)
- were Ian is going to have to spend more time (3.18)

Ethiopia - it's not Guatemala! (8.4)
Europe
- where Andrew is supposedly backpacking (2.23)
- poster visible in Tom's office (1.20)
- where Preston is coming home from (6.17)
- where Preston was (6.22)
- six months here would be educational (5.23)
- where Juanita was told Carlos went on business (8.13)
- where Preston is going (6.10)
- where Va Va Va Vroom is popular (7.6)

Eastern Pennsylvania - where the showers are moving through to the west (8.15)
England - where all the crap happened (8.4)
Everland - mayoral race results for this area can be seen on the television (3.21)
Emerson Woods - where Mike, Dave and Katherine went camping (5.18)
Fenway Park - Travers names his dog after this place (3.21)
Finland - where Bob and Lee flew to for their sculpture (4.5)
Florida
- where Danielle was going to go to college (4.5)
- where this is a biker who now has to puree all his food (5.6
- where a body was identified as Reggie (5.19)
- where Carlos' company has a branch (6.8)
- where Eddie's mother isn't (6.22)
- where Amber and Charlie are flying back to tomorrow (7.15)

Fort Lauderdale - where Dale is on Spring Break (2.19)
Ferndale - where Susan didn't come to a complete stop (7.15)
Florence - where Bree thought Orson got the mask (5.22)
Foster Lake - where Bree and Gaby should go next weekend (7.19)
Granville Field - where Ida made the only unassisted triple play in league history (4.10)
Greendale - where Tom has to drive to pick up napkins (3.12)

Greenwood - where Mike has a job (2.5)
Greece - where Carlos and Gaby bought the painting (5.10)
Georgia - where Hurricane Bell was off the coast (7.6)
Guatemala - is the answer (8.4)
Hamptons - where Zach owns a cottage (3.12)
Hawaii
- where Anabel is going in three days (1.22)
- where Eli is heading to after this job (5.13)
- where Tom planned the family vacation (7.21)

Hawkins Lake (8.6)
Hibiscus Circle - $20 in a cab only gets you this far (7.2)
Hilldale - where Charles is speaking at a conference (3.21)
Honolulu - were Marcy is (3.5)
Holland - where Penny wanted wooden shoes from (6.17)
Italy
- Milan
    o where Gaby worked the catwalks (3.9)
    o where Durkin shot Gaby (3.8)
    o where Gaby got a high fashion gown shipped from (2.17)
    o where Susan's shoes were made from the top couturier (6.1)
    o where Virginia is going to see the couture collections (5.6)
    o Grace walked the sidewalk like she was on a runway here (7.6)
        where Orson brought the Cashmere for Bree (8.14)
- Naples
    o where Ricks grandmother came over from (3.18)
    o where Rex and Bree went on vacation before the kids were born (1.21)
    o where Rex sweat like a pig and wished they hadn't spent all their savings (1.21)
    o where Rick just got back from (4.12)

- o where Rick learned to make Carbonara (3.19)
- o where the Maserati leather was imported from (1.20)
- o where the guy pressed charges after Irina cleared out his bank account (6.19)
- Venice
  - o where Orson actually got the mask (5.22)
  - o where Renee always stays in the suite (7.1)

Idaho - where Paul and Mike are not driving to (7.14)

Indianapolis- where Mike was always trying to get Carlos to go for a game (8.17)

Iran - it isn't Canada (5.22)

Iraq
- where Richard traipsed through (7.8)
- where a woman's husband is not fighting for our freedom (8.18)

Jamaica - where Austin's mother came back with new boobs and a cabin boy (3.2)

Japan
- where Yao Lin is not from (1.4)
- where clients are flying in from (8.17)

Kangwon Province - where 242 unsaved souls would be without Reverend Green (4.16)

Kenya
- where Gaby is concerned about the drought (2.10)
- where it was amazing (3.21)

Kerrigan Park - where Rashi is leading a meditation seminar (8.3)

Korea
- the first time it was a little rough, before you develop a taste for blood (8.14)
- where Roy came close to being a lady (7.8)
- where Roy served (7.18)

Los Angeles – where Mike moved from (1.10)

Laughlin - where Karen came home to find her husband dead (3.20)

Lake pleasant - where Peter has a summer place (5.6)
Lakeview - where Orson tells Bree his mother is in a home (3.8)
Las Colinas - where nobody apart from Gaby has ever been famous (7.15)
Levittown, Long Island - where Herbert is from (8.3)
Littleton - where Carlos is driving out to (7.18)
London - where Jane suggested she and Tom pop over to (8.12)
Los Colinas - where Gaby stirred things up again (7.23)
Louisville - where Bree joined a club for conservative women (8.23)
Las Vegas
- where Turk isn't no more (3.2)
- where Dave was at a real estate convention (5.1)
- where Stella lost money (5.12)
- would be cheaper (2.13)
- where Karl wants to take Bree (6.3)
- where Mike and Katherine are getting married (5.24)
- the vibe Lynette is getting (7.15)
- where Rashi should take his act (8.3)

Mansfield - where funnel clouds have been spotted (4.9)
Maryland - where Dylan is with her husband (5.6)
Miami - where Terrance took the job (6.12)
Middlebury, Vermont - where Orson went to school (3.10)
Minnesota
- where Jeannie is visiting her mother (2.5)
- where Orson is licensed as a dentist

Montana - where one of the camps is, that Bree wants to send Andrew to (1.17)
Montreal
- where Ian has to catch that plane to (3.13)
- where Tom has to get to tonight on the jet (7.18)

Mount Pleasant
- where Orson has a hotel room (4.14)
- where George is going to a bonsai exposition (1.20)
- where Paul has to go to for work today (1.16)

- where a tornado just hit (4.9)
- where some guy has a cracked water heater (3.23)
- mayoral race results for this area can be seen on the television (3.21)
- where Andrew is buying some end tables (5.9)
- where Gaby is not schlepping so Juanita can be with 'those people' (6.12)
- where Mike's sister lives (8.19)

Madrid - where Preston and Irina went (6.17)
Maine
- where Orson's aunt recently passed and left her coastal cabin to him (8.14)
- where Orson's cottage is right on the coast (8.15)

Maryland- where the war reenactors are getting ready to retreat into (7.16)
Mongolia - where there is a mother older than Lynette (6.3)
Mumbai
- where Tom is getting sent for a year (8.20)\
- where Tom is going for a year (8.21)

Mexico
- Guadalajara - where both Carlos and Gaby's family comes from (2.17)
- Tijuana- where Nora will be dancing in a nightclub (3.7)
- where Carlos and Gaby's ancestors come from (6.12)
- there is no way in hell Austin is heading there (3.2)
- where Hector is staying with his cousins (7.9)
- Karen lost her passports on the way here (8.22)
- where Susan's feet got sunburnt (5.24)
- where they will have Hector on a bus back to by tomorrow (7.8)

Micronesia - where Sam spent his summer digging wells (6.18)
Nebraska - where Ida's niece is taking all her stuff back to (4.10)
Newhaven - where the police have been working on the case for months (7.23)

New York
- where Gaby had been a model (2.23)
- where Lee's mother lives (6.19)
- where Gaby left a week after being molested by Alejandro (1.9)
- where Gaby lived out her modelling days (1.1)
- where Gaby is trying to send Danielle (1.7)
- where Gaby had designer shoes shipped from (2.17)
- where Deidre's body washed up in the toy chest (1.18)
- where Tom is (2.17)
- where Gaby is flying to meet her old agent (3.8)
- where Ana will get discovered (6.1)
- where the Bolens are from (6.3)
- where ANA is going to become a model (6.13)
- where Ana is going (6.15)
- where Danny went to find Ana (6.16)
- where Gaby bought a bus ticket to (1.9)
- where most of the anniversary party are coming in from (6.7)
- where Angie is on the way to (6.17)
- where Danny is going (6.23)
- where Renee flies Lynette out to every now and then (7.1)
- the style that Renee shops (8.16)
- where Gaby feels most at home (7.15)
- where Katherine wants Lynette to head the US division (8.23)
- where Renee has a friend who is a costume designers (8.6)
- where Renee is back from (7.5)
- where Susan is going (8.10)
- where Susan's skinny little toosh needs to be moved to (8.9)
- where Tom and Lynette got caught in a torrential downpour (8.18)
- where doug flew in from (7.5)

- where every stripper will tell you that Doug was a good guy (8.9)

North Korea - where the Reverend Michael Green smuggled bibles in (4.16)

Nagasaki - they never saw it coming (8.6)

Nice, France - where Preston saw Irina on the topless beach (6.17)

Oakdale - where Alex's mother made the long drive down from (5.11)

Ohio
- where Susan had a penpal (1.9)
- where Bob and Lee's child was (6.16)

Omaha - where Ida is being put in the family plot (4.10)

Oregon
- where they are going to clear cut 4000 acres of old growth (6.22)
- where Angie is going with Patrick to (6.23)

Ohio - where Miss Charlotte saw Mrs. Humphries in a window in a tiny shop (7.12)

Oklahoma
- where Ramone Sanchez was living (8.10)
- where Susan decided to fly to visit the Sanchez family (8.12)
- where the missing guy is from (8.8)

Palestine - Bree's suggestion for a control word (1.14)

Paris
- where Bradley proposed to Dylan under the Eiffel Tower (4.17)
- where Gaby worked the catwalks (3.9)
- where Gaby's gets her exotic perfume shipped from (2.17)
- where Jackson went to art school (5.7)
- where Walter is thinking of going (4.10)
- where you can practically make love anywhere (3.4)
- where Gabys clothes are from (1.2)
- where Mike can't afford to fly Susan to (3.23)

- where Susan isn't going (3.7)
- where Virginia is going to see the couture collections (5.6)
- the greatest city in the world (5.16)
- where Ana will get discovered (6.1)
- where Preston and Irina went (6.17)
- where Robyn has always wanted to see (6.18)
- where Gaby has been (7.15)
- where Jane spent a couple of semesters (8.6)
- where tom and jane are heading (8.9)
- where Lynette thinks Tom should go (8.10)
- the power had to go off when Tom was there (8.11)
- where Tom is not back from yet (8.12)
- where it's hard to tell the difference between men and women (8.23)

Prague - where Preston and Irina went (6.17)

Philadelphia
- where Bree's Aunt Fern lives (1.14)
- where Bree tells Andrew and Danielle that Rex is at a medical conference (1.4)

Pinewood Valley State Forest - where Mike is hiking to the Hot Springs (3.21)

Pennsylvania - where Chuck was born (7.21)

Portland - where Dave is going on a speaking tour (5.22)

Riverton
- where Jackson went to visit his old art professor (5.11)
- where jackson got a teaching job at a college (5.12)

Rio - a month here would be so romantic (4.7)

Romania - where Katherine found Dylan #2 in an orphanage (4.17)

Rhode Island
- this state can fit into Alaska 424 times (7.7)
- where Bree's father and stepmother are going to take Andrew (2.19)

Rwanda - where Father Dugan will be digging wells for lepers (8.1)

Rome
- a trip here would be so romantic (2.13)
- where Ian's parents are (3.13)
- where Virginia needs to go for two months (5.6)
- where Gaby has been (7.15)

Russia
- where Edie wants Dave to head over to at the alcohol store (5.16)
- where it's every mother's dream to see the inside of a cow (6.18)

Rockwater Lake
- where police recovered a chest (1.3)
- where the toy chest was pulled out of (1.9)
- where the toy chest washed up (2.15)
- where Betty and Caleb are going on a picnic (2.21)

Royal Oaks - the scene of a hate crime (1.4)
San Francisco - where Tom has to go back in the morning (1.1)
Saint Barthélemy
- where Carlos had his hands over Gaby's naughty bits (2.16)
- where Carlos took Lucy to celebrate her first promotion (5.17)
- the pool cleaner can clean Renee's pool on Wednesday if he is back here by then (7.17)

Scotland - where Edie wants Dave to start looking for alcohol (5.16)
Southern Alps - where Bree sent Gaby a basket of muffins from (3.20)
Sri Lanka - where there was a catastrophic flood (2.8)
Seattle - where Dave is going on a speaking tour (5.22)
Sequoia National Forest - one of the stops on Lynette's proposed vacation (7.21)
South America - where Richard wants to sail down the coast by himself (7.8)
South of France

- where Bradley picked his wine up on a wine tasting trip (8.11)
- where Gaby needs a good hotel (8.5)

Sydney - where Mr. Faulkner is on a one way flight back to, if Renee doesn't comply with the prosecution (8.22)

Switzerland
- where Zach Young owns a chateau (3.12)
- where Bree and Orson ran across a boarding school (3.23)
- where Danielle is at boarding school (3.23, 4.4)
- where Danielle is driving back to tomorrow (4.6)
- where Tammy Brennan would order specialists before she would cancel (1.16)
- where Prestons brother wanted an army knife from (6.17)

Sogamore, Connecticut - where Orson stayed in a mental hospital (3.10)

Torch Lake - where Edie and Susan go to scatter Martha's ashes (1.12)

Tahiti - where Gaby tells the Father he can take a trip with her donation (6.8)

Texas
- where Carmen and Grace are going to stay (7.9)
- where Carmen has relatives (7.8)
- where Gaby doesn't want to fly to stand on a dead guy's grave and read a letter (7.15)

The Bronx - where the Reverend Sikes was driven to a bad part of town (7.16)

The Holland Tunnel - what Bree feels like (7.5)

The Grand Canyon - one of the stops on Lynette's proposed vacation (7.21)

The Red Sea (6.8) - Gaby is not asking 'padre' to part this

The Soviet Union - the globe is from before this broke up (6.6)

The Tropics - where Howard dreams of retiring (1.17)

The Bahamas - where Edie and Dave went (5.13)

Tibet - where monks remember 'the pie thing' (4.12)

Tucson
- where Carlos's cousin is (3.18)
- where Lynette had a 104 fever, but still managed to take the kids trick or treating (2.1)
- where Mason's dad is moving his family to (2.16)

Utah
- where Zack took a bus to (2.6)
- a little too conservative for Edie (1.16)
- where Felicia and Angela worked together (1.18)
- where Paul might be (2.4)
- where Susan helped Zach go (2.4, 2.5)
- where the death penalty is (1.22)

Valley Ridge - where its too close to call (3.21)

Valley View Park - where Lynette scores some high grade nanny (1.9)

Virginia
- where Orson did prison dental work (2.24)
- where Stacey's family lives (7.3)

Washington - where Victor is (4.6)

Webster - where funnel clouds have been spotted (4.9)

Wisteria Park - where the romantic moment, wasn't so romantic (8.18)

Wyoming - where the historical birch came from (7.2)

Whitman's Bluff - where the horse drawn carriage will take Tom and Lynette (3.16)

Winnipeg - where Alma was with a deaf aunt and no credit (3.11)

Yalu River - where it glimmers like Bree's eyes on a moonlit night (4.16)

Zimbabwe - where Edna Fletcher was lounging around in the peace corps (4.11)

Zurich - where Gaby can get non FDA approved diet pills from her friends (3.9)

"HOW MUCH DO WE REALLY WANT TO KNOW ABOUT OUR NEIGHBOURS?"

TRIVIA

General

- The show was rejected by Lifetime and HBO
- Teri Hatcher is the first person to win the SAG-AFTRA award for Outstanding Performance in a Comedy Series, for a show that hadn't even completed its first season
- Marcia Cross originally auditioned for the role of Mary Alice, and Nicollette Sheridan and Laura Leighton auditioned for Bree. In addition, Dana Delany was originally considered for the part of Bree but turned the role down three times. Calista Flockhart, Heather Locklear, Courtney Cox, and Mary-Louise Parker were considered for the role of Susan. Roselyn Sanchez was considered for the role of Gabrielle, but lost the role at final audition rounds.
- Ricardo Chavira was almost not cast as Carlos, as producers believed he was too young
- Bree is based on Marc Cherry's mother, as is the idea for the pilot. She once told him that she often felt 'desperate' when she was raising her family, and even spoke Bree's iconic line to Andrew, "I'd love you even if you were a murderer"
- The only actors to appear in every episode are Teri Hatcher, Felicity Huffman, and Eva Longoria
- Every episode except the pilot is named after a Stephen Sondheim song, or lyrics
- Almost every time a newspaper is shown, it is the same one
- Only two episodes of the show are not narrated by Mary-Alice, 3.16 and 5.19
- Other titles for the show were considered including *The Secret Lives of Housewives,* and *The Secrets of Wisteria Lane*

- Marc Cherry considered the show to be a mix of *Knots Landing, American Beauty,* and *Twin Peaks*

Season One

1.1
- It took almost two weeks to shoot the pilot episode
- The gown that Gabrielle wears while mowing the lawn was loaned to a student from Saint Hubert Roman Catholic High School in Philadelphia. Melissa Saunders wrote to the producers of the show and asked for photos of the dress so that she could find a similar outfit to wear to her senior prom. The show instead sent her the original dress, having even added a lining so that it would comply with the modesty requirements of the school
- The envelope from Mary Alice's blackmail note reads "Secretsville, USA"
- The Van de Kamp family dinner was the first scene to be filmed
- This is the second pilot to be filmed. The first had different casting including Sheryl Lee as Mary Alice, Michael Reilly Burke as Rex, and Kyle Searles as John
- Sheryl Lee was replaced with Brenda Strong, as the creators of the show felt that the narration needed a more comic tone
- The Scavo children's names all start with the letter "P", following in the tradition of Lynette whose sisters are Lucy and Lydia
- The women say that the postmark indicates that Mary Alice must have received the letter on the day that she died, but a postmark only indicates when the postal service receives the mail, not the delivery
- The co-worker that Lynette bumps into at the grocery store is seen twice again throughout the series, including in the very last episode

- Wisteria Lane had several dogs which disappeared over time. Mike, Bob, Roy, and Parker all had dogs that stopped appearing without explanation
- When Bree is standing in front of Edie's house watching the fire, she turns to go talk to Rex, who is the original Rex - Michael Reilly Burke
- In the first season, Tom was originally supposed to cheat on Lynette
- The pilot broke records for most-watched episode

1.2

- In Mike's map, Lynette and Tom's baby is labeled "Daisy"
- John's underwear is visible under his towel, but then is missing when he is pushed out of the window

1.4

- The blackmail note was clearly crumpled and creased in earlier episodes, but here seems almost perfectly smooth

1.7

- Lynette's idea to put advertising on dry-cleaning bags was used to promote the show. ABC had "everyone has a little dirty laundry" put onto thousands of dry cleaning bags

1.9

- During the fashion show, when Tom is announcing Susan, you can see his mouth is not moving

1.13

- At the school dance, the students are clearly dancing to a fast song, but a slow one is playing, suggesting that the music was dubbed over after filming

1.15
- When Carlos signs the Valentine's card, it is clear that he is left-handed
- Karen said she bought the plant pot in Costa Rica, but the price says p200. The currency in Costa Rica is the Colone which would read ¢.

1.16
- Juanita would not be able to walk around the hospital ward like that after so many months in a coma
- When Tom signs "I love you", he actually signs "Mine love you"

1.18
- When Lynette is in the bathroom telling the kids off about their toothbrushes, you can see her talking in the mirror, with no sound coming out

1.20
- It is revealed in this episode that Lynette's maiden name is Lindquist

1.21
- At lunch, bree appears to be wearing Maisy's pearl choker
- When Susan sees Mike from across the street grabbing his mail, this is repeated footage from 1.19
- When Morty proposes, you can see the top of the set without the ceiling

1.23

- Rex was killed off because Marc Cherry's father died
- The calender shows March 1, 1990 as a Wednesday, but in reality that was a Thursday

Season Two

2.4
- Gaby is meant to be pregnant, but is seen drinking wine at Bree's

2.8
- This is the first episode showing the re-cast Caleb

2.11
- This is the first time that we learn that Carlos is secretly attracted to Lynette throughout the show

2.15
- The opera singer's lip movements do not quite match the tune of her song
- It is the weekend and Valentine's day, but in 2006 when the episode is set according to the calendar in 2.17, Valentine's was a Tuesday

2.16
- The handwriting on Bree's calendar changes between shots. It starts out capitalised, then is written in cursive, and misspelled as "Februay"

2.17
- Veronica's son's lip movements don't match up when he is telling her that he is thirsty
- A boom mic is visible in the car window when Deanna is leaving the Solis house

2.23
- The finale aired as a 2-hour special on ABC, but in two parts internationally

Season Three

3.2
- Gaby has slip guards on her shoes which disappear and reappear between shots
- Orson uses the wrong side of his pocket knife to cut the ropes on his car

3.7
- Matt Roth who plays Art, was once married to Laurie Metcalfe who plays Caroline
- Marcia Cross is pregnant in real life, and from this episode onwards, various shots and props are used to cover her growing abdomen

3.8
- The shirt that Art wears to prove he is "Protector Man" is not the Purdue logo, or colors

3.15
- Kyle Maclachlan (Orson) said that the fight scene between himself and Dixie Carter (Gloria) required no stunt doubles, as she had such a strong physique

3.16
- Marcia Cross takes maternity leave from now until the end of the season, making this the first episode of the show that Bree is not in. Her appearance at the beginning of this episode is a stand-in.
- This is the first of only two episodes in the series that are not narrated by Brenda Strong. This one is narrated by Steven Culp (Rex)

3.23
- This is Bree's first appearance since Marcia's maternity leave

Season Four

4.1
- Gaby's lipstick is a different shade than in her wedding in the previous season

4.2
- Gaby asks Edie what she wants for her birthday but we know from 3.21 that Edie's birthday was several weeks earlier
- A crew person's head can be seen in the window when Bree walks out of the Mayfair's kitchen door

4.4
- Bob and Lee are named after American journalist Bob Woodruff and his wife Lee

4.5
- Danielle states that she will be turning 18 in the weekend. In 2.22, she was said to have turned 17 one month prior, which would make her closer to 19.

4.6
- The genetic counselor Susan that she was 26 when she was pregnant with Julie. That would make Susan around 44-45, but we know from 2.10 that Susan would only be turning 40 this season

4.7
- The Scavo children's names all start with the letter "P". It is clear from this episode that Lynette has done this in line with her own family tradition, as her sister's names all start with "L".

4.8
- The pills that Gaby uses to spike Carlos' drink are labeled as Doryx, which is known as Doxycycline, an antibiotic, not a sedative.

4.10
- This was the last episode written before the famous writer's strike, and was written in a way that it could serve as an early season finale if need be

4.14
- When Kayla is talking to Lynette, you can see a man in a blue shirt in the mirror behind Lynette

4.17
- This is the final episode of the fourth season, which makes it the shortest season out of the whole show. It was shortened due to the Writer's Guild of America strike.
- This is the only episode with the original Juanita. From Season 5, Juanita is played by Madison De La Garza.

Season Five

5.1
- This episode reflects a five year time jump since the events of the season 4 finale
- Juanita is said to be only four years old, but Madison De La Garza who plays her was actually six at the time

5.8
- The opening for this episode says that someone will be arrested, but nobody does get arrested

5.12
- The on-screen credit for Marcia Cross is missing from the opening credits of this episode, which was a breach of Marcia's contract. The credit was later added to the DVD release

5.13
- This marks the show's 100th episode
- Martha Huber's appearance is different from the pilot where she discovered Mary Alice's body
- This episode reveals that Eli was the last person to see Mary Alice alive
- In this episode, Susan asks Eli to change the locks after Karl leaves. However, in Season 2, we see Karl telling Julie that he still has the key to the house, and uses it to let himself in
- Eli accidentally informs Susan that Karl has been cheating on her with more women than just Brandy, However, in 1.11, Susan finds out for the first time that Karl cheated on her with more than one woman

- When Gaby goes to Lynette's house, it has a picket fence, even though this wasn't added until several seasons into the show
- Lynette's treehouse is also visible, though this wouldn't have been built at this time
- Susan's dining area is shown in flashbacks, even though this wasn't built until after the fire in her house
- The paint color inside Lynette's house is inconsistent with earlier scenes. It was pink at the start of the show, but in the flashbacks it is blue
- This is the first of four episodes in the series which centers on one character (Eli)

5.14

- Bree brags about how she just bought her new car, but she has been seen driving it for several episodes
- Bree brags about how her car's refrigerator can fit champagne and chilled glasses, yet she is a recovering alcoholic

5.18

- Nicolette Sheridan was written out of the series under debatable circumstances. Marc Cherry claimed it was a creative decision, while Sheridan filed a claim in court for wrongful dismissal.

5.19

- This is the second and final episode of the series to be voiced over by a character other than Mary Alice
- When the tire blows out on the car, Susan asks if anybody knows how to changes tire, but in 1.12 we see Susan changing Edie's
- This is the second of four episodes in the series which centers on one character (Edie)

Season Six

6.1
- It was originally March Cherry's intention for Mike and Katherine to get married, but he changed his mind after he saw the fan reactions for the upcoming season
- The veil that was covering Mike's bride at the end of Season 5 is different to the one that Susan wears in this episode
- In this episode, Susan becomes the second character to marry the same man twice (Gaby was the first)

6.4
- This is the last episode we see John Rowland appear in

6.8
- When Bree is talking to Angie in her bedroom orange marking tape is visible on the floor

6.10
- Orson accuses Carl of trying to represent Bree in the divorce. Orson has already been served divorce papers, so if Carl was representing Bree, Orson would already know about it

6.15
- This is the third of four episodes in the series which centers on one character (Robin0

6.17

- Supermodel Heidi Klum makes an appearance in this episode

6.18
- Sam is said to be 26, but this doesn't add up. If Rex were still alive, he would have been married to Bree for 28 years by this episode, meaning Sam would have to be closer to 30 for Rex to have conceived him before he married Bree

6.20
- This is the fourth and final episode in the series which centers on one character (Eddie)
- This is the only appearance of Mary-Alice in season 6
- This episode has parallels to Alfred Hitchcock's *Psycho*

6.22
- In the flashback of Angie in college, the periodic table of the elements is visible. The chart is inaccurate though as it contains six elements that were not named until the late 1990s, years after this alleged scene takes place

6.23
- Mark Moses' on-screen credit was not showing, in order to keep his return a secret until the final seconds of the episode
- Marc Cherry was asked by the ABC chairman to write Katherine out of the show, to free actress Dana Delany up to star in *Body of Proof*

Season Seven

7.1
- After four seasons on Ugly Betty, Vanessa Williams was cast in Desperate Housewives as her ABC contract still had two more years

7.2
- Bree says her track record with men is two dead, one in a wheelchair. Bree has had three men from her serious relationships die, so it's not clear which two she is referring to (Rex, George, Karl).

7.6
- It is revealed in this episode that Tom has two siblings, Peter, and Teresa

7.7
- Mary Alice's narration in this episode reveals that Karen and Roy got married

7.18
- Most scenes in this episode don't take place on Wisteria Lane
- Felicia Tilman's "amputated fingers" can be seen in this episode

Season Eight

8.1
- Gaby says she drove a manual transmission car in high school once, but we saw her drive one in 7.8

8.2
- This is Mark Moses' final appearance on the show

8.4
- Final appearance of Joy Lauren

8.6
- Tony Plana, who plays Alejandro directed this episode
- Lynette can't sew a costume for Penny, yet she sewed all of the costumes for the Barcliff school play in Season 1

8.10
- The motel room Bree is in, is the same one where she would meet Karl

8.11
- In 8.9. Chuck says that Ramon has two daughters, but we see only one in this episode
- There is a 20-year age gap between Tony Plana who plays Alejandro, and Justina Machado (Claudia Sanchez)
- Susan's cheque says "4353 Wisteria Lane, Fairview, ES 00057"

8.13

- This episode marks the least watched episode of the series

8.14
- The end of this episode is narrated by Orson

8.15
- Final appearance of Orson
- In the flashback, the Scavo boys are played by different actors than those in the first four seasons of the series

8.16
- There is a crew member visible in the side view mirror, when Bree is talking to Karen

8.17
- In this episode, Susan becomes the third wife to be widowed in the series

8.19
- The seal in the courtroom behind the judge is dated 1876, indicating that the show is set in Colorado - the only state admitted to the union in 1876

8.23
- Marc Cherry, in the DVD commentary, said that he originally wrote Trip as running for office, and Bree becoming first lady. Marcia Cross requested that this be changed, and that her character go into politics
- This episode was the most watched series finale in 2012
- Carmen, the new gardener for the Solis' is a character in the spin off show *Devious Maids*
- Kathryn Joosten battled lung cancer in real life, and passed away just 20 days after this episode aired
- Marc Cherry has a cameo in this episode as the moving man

References and Credits

Opening Sequence Artwork
- All images from Desperate Housewives Wiki

Mikes Map
- Image used from Ebay

Simplified and edited version of map from Behind Closed Doors
- Image from Cherry Marc Number Seventeen (Firm) Downtown Bookworks Inc Touchstone Television and American Broadcasting Company. 2005. *Desperate Housewives : Behind Closed Doors*. New York: Hyperion : ABC : Touchstone Television. https://archive.org/details/desperatehousewi00cher.

Ants in my picnic basket
- Image used from https://mobile.twitter.com/_SusanMayer

Martha Huber Poster
Alejandro Poster
Renee and Ben Wedding Invitation
Oakridge Pamphlet
Oakridge Talent Show
Meyer Family Photos
Melanie Foster Crime Scene Photos and Note
Va Va Va Broom Payslip
- Images used from Ebay Seller: **justasmalltownboy13x**

Mike and Susan Wedding Order of Events
Susan Kidney Poster
- Image used from Worthpoint

Bree Cookbook:
- https://br.pinterest.com/pin/290482244717824237/?nic_v3=1a7dNZQpQ

Bree Office Wall Covers and Articles
- Image used from natedsanders.com

Driver License Collage
- Image used from Reddit

1. Akass K, McCabe J (Janet E. *Reading Desperate Housewives : Beyond the White Picket Fence* . Edited by Janet McCabe & Kim Akass. First edition. I.B. Tauris & Co. Ltd; 2019.
2. Coward, Rosalind (2006), 'Still Desperate: Popular Television and the Female Zeitgeist', in Janet McCabe and Kim Akass (eds.), *Reading Desperate Housewives: Beyond the White Picket Fence,* London, I.B. Tauris, pp. 31-41.

About the Author

Ko Takitumu, ko Hikurangi ōku māunga
Ko Aparima, ko Waiapu ōku awa
Ko Horouta, ko Mataatua ōku waka
Ko Kāi Tahu, ko Ngāti Pōrou, ko Kāti Māmoe ōku iwi
Ko te Aowera, ko Te Aitanga a mate ōku hapū
Nō Otepoti ahau, Kei Tauranga e noho ana
Ko Allen Harris rāua ko Debra Constable ōku mātua
Ko Jonny-ray ratou ko Ciara, ko Nathan, ko Alex aku tamariki
Ko Ciara ratou ko Nathan, ko Alex. He whāngai ratou
Ko Stephen Dryfhout taku hoa rangatira
Ko Taryn Dryfhout tōku ingoa

Taryn is an experienced writer, teacher, theologian, and coffee junkie who lives in New Zealand with her husband and four children.

A Rory-inspired blue-stocking, Taryn is a serial student, earning several diplomas and degrees, and now currently completing a PhD program. She works as a college tutor, and has won awards for her postgraduate research and Māori leadership.

Taryn has written several non-fiction books, tertiary college courses, website content, and more than 400 feature articles, reviews, and columns published in newspapers, websites, and magazines. She has been nominated for "Best Feature Writer" and "Best Columnist", and is a member of Mensa, the NZ Society of Authors, and NZ Christian Writers.

When Taryn is not writing, studying, teaching, or with her kids, she can be found reading books, buying books, or watching her favourite television shows.

www.TarynDryfhout.com

www.ingramcontent.com/pod-product-compliance
Lightning Source LLC
Chambersburg PA
CBHW051421290426
44109CB00016B/1384